CW00548793

THE MR PORTER PAPERBACK
VOLUME THREE

THE
MR
PORTER
PAPER-
BACK

THE MANUAL FOR
A STYLISH
LIFE

VOLUME THREE

 Thames & Hudson

First published in the United Kingdom in 2014 by
Thames & Hudson Ltd, 181A High Holborn, London WC1V 7QX
by arrangement with Net-A-Porter Group Ltd

The MR PORTER Paperback vol.3 © 2014 Net-A-Porter Group Ltd

British Library Cataloguing-in-Publication Data
A catalogue record for this book is available from the
British Library

ISBN 978-0-500-29152-8

Printed and bound in China by Toppan Leefung Printing, Ltd

To find out about all our publications, please visit
www.thamesandhudson.com. There you can subscribe
to our e-newsletter, browse or download our
current catalogue, and buy any titles that are in print.

CONTENTS

FOREWORD

WHETHER IT IS Mr Gianni Agnelli skiing in Sestriere, Italy or
Mr David Bowie taking the stage in his Ziggy Stardust finery,
each of us has a style icon we channel when we get ready to face
the day. Our choice of fragrance may be all that remains of an old
flame's attempt to refurbish us. The cut of our suit? A homage to
a dashing uncle or early mentor. The car we drive may be a present
that we have been waiting to give ourselves since we first spotted
a Karmann Ghia screeching around a corner as a boy.

We are the sum of these parts.

Here at MR PORTER, we view these bits of stylistic DNA much
the way early explorers viewed certain constellations; they are our
guiding lights that allow us to set sail for uncharted lands. The
book you hold in your hand is our attempt to provide you with
what those ancient mariners called a sextant – a navigation device
that should either reaffirm the course you're on or allow you to
borrow a move from some of the most stylish men on the planet.

Like most of the successes at MR PORTER, this book was put
together by a backing band every bit as glam as The Spiders from
Mars including Production Editor Ms Xanthe Greenhill, Editorial
Coordinator Ms Caroline Hogan, Sub-Editor Ms Siân Morgan,
Art Director Mr Eric Åhnebrink and Editor Ms Jodie Harrison. To
understand from whence Ms Harrison's cheeky charm originates
merely turn to page 142 to read her dad's thoughts on the proper
way to court the love of your life (hint: it involves a whistle).

Mr John Brodie, Editor-in-Chief

"To do a dull thing with style is preferable to doing a dangerous thing without it. To do a dangerous thing with style is what I call art."

Mr Charles Bukowski

HOW TO GET YOUR IDEA OFF THE GROUND

Strike while the iron is hot to create a dynamic new business

Words by Mr Henry Farrar-Hockley

THERE'S NO TIME like the present to launch a start-up, with low setup costs and high demand for new businesses benefiting fledgling entrepreneurs. Plus you can dictate your own "office" hours and kiss goodbye to the daily commute. But you needn't take our word for it: Microsoft, Disney, IBM and Apple were all founded during periods of global financial turmoil – and some of those guys have done OK.

Entrepreneurs are clearly buying into this logic: in 2013 a record 502,068 start-ups were established in the UK, while in the US 476,000 new businesses were launched each month. Of course, turning your big idea into an even bigger success will require a significant amount of patience, planning and caffeine – not to mention outside help, which is why we've called on the expertise of five start-up gurus who've been there and done that.

I

DON'T FIXATE ON BEING FIRST

Don't waste precious time trying to come up with a never-seen-before product, feature or service. It's not frowned upon to improve rather than invent. "Originality should take a back seat to relevance," explains Mr Steve McGrath, a veteran angel investor and partner at innovation consultancy Strategos. "From a strategy perspective, being first to market with an idea is by no means a guarantee of success. What is essential is identifying and validating an unmet need." Facebook didn't coin social networking and Dropbox wasn't the first to offer file hosting. These start-ups simply knew how to make their products more efficient – and a hell of a lot more appealing – than everyone else's.

2
SHARE YOUR IDEAS

You don't need to be the CEO of LinkedIn Mr Jeff Weiner to know that networking is an essential asset for the first-time entrepreneur, but this is as much about gaining valuable insights on your product as opening doors. "A lot of first-time entrepreneurs worry that if they share their idea, they're exposing themselves to having it stolen so they don't tell anyone about it," says Mr Jacob Gibson, founder of consumer money advisor NerdWallet, "but unless you have an invention worth patenting, just focus on execution. By sharing your idea with others, you get the benefit of their advice, and validation for whether or not your idea is workable."

3
BUILD A TEAM

Even the most intelligent, driven innovators need a dedicated team to help bring their idea to fruition, and the more inquisitive your colleagues the better. "The best advice I could give is to surround yourself with the smartest people you can find," Mr McGrath says. "Intel has an expression that describes how it operates. It's known as 'constructive confrontation' and it cuts across the whole hierarchy. Basically it looks for people to really push each other around intellectually." The same goes for your start-up: the more you and your team can question your product, the closer you'll be to that billion-dollar valuation.

GET YOUR PRODUCT OUT THERE

Another common mistake is thinking your product needs to be perfected before you can bring it to market. In truth, the customer won't care too much about the sans serif typeface you've chosen for the packaging – they just want to know if it works for them. "You don't really know you've hit on a great idea until you see market feedback," says Mr Eric Kuhn, CEO of FoundersCard, a global membership community of entrepreneurs and innovators. "Start off with a small test market and stay very close to customer response."

5
CHOOSE YOUR INVESTORS WISELY

When approaching investors remember that capital is only one part of the equation. "It isn't like going to an ATM," explains Mr McGrath. "The relationship you're about to set up with an investor is essentially like dating: it's deeply intimate, so you want to know who you're dealing with." "Early on, it's as much about you as it is about your harebrained business idea," adds Mr Greg Marsh, founder of high-end property rental service onefinestay, "so your personal credibility (that is, what people really say about you behind your back) is tremendously important. The best way that credibility is conveyed is through your network, and how far it's willing to go for you."

6
GET YOURSELF HEARD

With so many marketing channels to choose from – from organic search to social media – you need to identify who your audience is and which platforms to engage them on. Although you could just meet up with them instead. "We found that holding open house events at our offices with users we engaged via online forums worked very well for us," reflects Mr Jason Trost, founder and CEO of sports betting exchange Smarkets. "It doesn't cost much, and it's great to meet your target users face to face, talk about their experience with your product and gain feedback."

7
LEARN FAST

There's nothing wrong with making mistakes – the truth is you're going to make a lot of them along the way – just so long as you're able to learn from them quickly and adapt your model accordingly. "Always be learning," advises Mr Gibson. "This is one of our three core values: we hire based on an individual's ability to take smart risks, admit failures and learn from them. As simple as this sounds, it's completely opposed to the way we're all raised in school and work, where mistakes are frowned upon and everyone is looking for the right answer, rather than redefining the question." Last but not least it pays to heed the words of Sir Ian Holm in the 1996 motion picture *Big Night*: "I am a businessman. I am anything I need to be at any time."

MR RALPH FIENNES

The star of The Grand Budapest Hotel *reveals
his secret past in the hotel game*

Words by Mr Alex Bilmes, editor-in-chief of British *Esquire*

FOR SIX MONTHS IN 1983, as a stop-gap between finishing an art foundation course and starting his studies at RADA, Mr Ralph Fiennes, then aged 20, worked as a house porter at Brown's Hotel in Mayfair in London, changing shower curtains and light bulbs and performing other menial but essential tasks.

Mr Fiennes, who three decades later plays perhaps the most soulful, most effervescent hotel concierge in movie history in Mr Wes Anderson's madcap fancy, *The Grand Budapest Hotel*, tells me about his brief sojourn in the hospitality trade. It is a preamble to a story that illustrates something about the self-importance of certain senior hotel staff, as well as about the colourful characters he met during his time vacuuming the corridors at Brown's.

Here's the story, as Mr Fiennes tells it:

"I was polishing a glass chandelier outside the men's loo and Jeremy Irons appeared. He was becoming a big star with *Brideshead* [*Revisited*] at the time, and I loved *Brideshead*. He spoke first:

'I need to clean some glass at home. What are you using?'

I showed him some generic glass-cleaning product.

'Thank you very much,' he said.

I said, 'Excuse me, are you Jeremy Irons?'

He said, 'Yes.'

I said, 'Could I have your autograph?'

He said, 'Well, listen, I'll leave it for you at the front desk.'

I said, 'Oh, thank you very much.'

And then I finished polishing my chandelier and I went up to the front desk where the concierge – a very pompous man in a brown and gold braid uniform – looked down his nose at me, because I was the lowest of the low in my white house coat, and said (very curtly), 'What do you want?'

I said, 'Did Jeremy Irons leave an autograph for me?'

'Yes (even more curtly). Here it is.'

And he passed me a piece of Brown's notepaper. I opened it. It said, 'Dear Ralph, Keep polishing. Jeremy Irons.'"

Monsieur Gustave, the maverick concierge at The Grand Budapest Hotel, would not have approved, Mr Fiennes confirms, of a houseboy asking a celebrity for his autograph. Fastidious, moustachioed, liberally perfumed and clad in a purple frock coat, his parted hair streaked with blond, Gustave is a ladies' man with a difference – he likes them blonde, needy, rich and very, very elderly – as well as a stickler for process.

When we meet Mr Fiennes has a firm handshake and a sympathetic smile. Lean and youthful at 51, his is not, initially, an imposing presence. He is dressed in standard off-duty menswear – jeans, sweater, navy peacoat – and he has a dark beard, flecked with grey. His distinguishing features are his pale blue-green eyes, full of understanding, and that familiar, softly mellifluous voice.

We talk in an anteroom on a battered leather sofa, into which he first sinks and then shrinks, staring into the distance and appearing to almost evaporate from the room. I tell him that I'd watched *The Invisible Woman*, which he directed, having completed it just before he began work on *Budapest*. I wonder how he managed to achieve an atmosphere of such intimacy, and to bring such high emotion to what is, on the surface, such a measured, even reserved movie.

Quickly he comes to life, leaning towards me, eyes locked on mine, hands dancing, showing me how the camera is positioned, where the characters are placed in a scene. It's the word "intimacy" and the phrase "on the surface" that set him alight; in some sense, Mr Fiennes' career to date has been an attempt to see beneath the surface, or perhaps to use the surface to express depth.

The Invisible Woman is the story of the mature Mr Charles Dickens' affair with a young aspiring actress, Ms Nelly Ternan – an affair that poisoned Mr Dickens' marriage and threatened to ruin Ms Ternan's life. Mr Fiennes' Dickens is a monumental figure – a superstar, a magician, full of ferocious energy.

Mr Fiennes' debut as director, *Coriolanus* (2011), was twitchy, kinetic, shot in documentary style, but *The Invisible Woman* is much more delicate. The camera inches towards the characters just as they inch towards each other – falling in love "incrementally", to use Mr Fiennes' word for it.

He is a director discovering his own aesthetic: "There are tiny compositional moments in *Coriolanus* where I felt, 'This is what I like!' It's not just her face/ his face, it's what the frame is showing and what that can do as emotion, storytelling, character. I think I brought that excitement to *The Invisible Woman*."

On stage Mr Fiennes has worked with the finest directors of our time. He was Troilus for Mr Sam Mendes and Edmund in Mr Nicholas Hytner's *King Lear*. With the director Mr Jonathan Kent he has been Hamlet, Richard II and Coriolanus. Mr Fiennes has been Romeo, Prospero and *Julius Caesar*'s Mark Antony. He has acted in Chekhov, Ibsen, Beckett. It is a spectacular career.

On film, his international break was in Mr Steven Spielberg's *Schindler's List*, as the Nazi death camp commandant Amon Goeth. His first film as romantic lead was the late Mr Anthony Minghella's epic weepie *The English Patient*. Mr Fiennes is no snob: he was also Ms Jennifer Lopez's love interest in *Maid in Manhattan*; a psycho killer in *Red Dragon*; Hades in *Clash of the Titans*. He is an expert in the high-impact cameo: a cockney gangster in *In Bruges*; a British mercenary in *The Hurt Locker*; Mallory in *Skyfall*. Perhaps most famously he's Lord Voldemort in the *Harry Potter* films.

But grown-up cinemagoers will associate him chiefly with his intense, intelligent, fine-grained portraits of reticent, diffident men in extreme circumstances: the academic cheat in *Quiz Show*; the jealous lover in *The End of the Affair*; the bereaved diplomat in *The Constant Gardener*. Everyone, Mr Fiennes suggests, has a quiet man inside. And a dormant Voldemort, too. Or a cockney gangster. "I liked exploring Harry in *In Bruges*. I'm not a tough guy but everyone's got a bit of rage inside. If I'm offered a part like that it's exciting, it's a challenge – it's not what I normally get asked to do."

And neither is *The Grand Budapest Hotel*'s Gustave, another character he feels close to. "In a way he's sort of an actor," Mr Fiennes says. "He presents himself in his role of concierge. He inhabits it fully but I think underneath he's a rather lonely soul. Like a lot of performers who are defined by the moment when they are performing, and when they're not they're slightly adrift."

I tell Mr Fiennes I wrote the word "luvvie" to describe Gustave. He takes polite offence on his character's behalf. "That's a word that most actors refuse to utter. I detest it. I detest that expression." And, he says, it doesn't apply to Gustave, for all his vanity and his affectations. "Gustave's sense of principle is profoundly rooted and he's a man of honour and principle. Wes has written an unusual hero, a man who has a moral code, an unforced nobility."

I wonder if it wasn't difficult to fit into Mr Anderson's scheme, so precise are the worlds he creates. "Wes is incredibly precise," says Mr Fiennes. "But as an actor you learn to accept there's a kind of director you work with because they are auteurs. If you work with Wes Anderson you go knowing and wanting to be part of the thing they do. I loved trying to be part of his world." It sounds as if he had fun doing it, too. "Wes likes everyone to stay close," he says, "ideally in the same hotel. There were no individual trailers, and in the evening everyone gathered for a good meal. It's very civilised. I think Wes engenders a great warmth and a good spirit."

Stupidly, I didn't ask if any of the house porters asked for his autograph. I imagine if they did, he left it for them at the front desk.

FIFTY YEARS OF THE
PORSCHE 911

*MR PORTER pays tribute to one of the most
iconic silhouettes in motoring history*

Words by Mr Paul Henderson

"I COULDN'T FIND the car of my dreams," Mr Ferdinand "Ferry" Porsche once said. "So I built it." Fifty years and more than 820,000 cars later, and the German car giant is still building, improving and perfecting what has been described as the quintessential sports car. Despite all the success of the Porsche 911, however, it was a difficult birth.

Long before it was given its three-digit nomenclature, the 911 was merely a follow-up project to the company's first production car, the 356. First unveiled in 1948, the 356 was a lightweight rear-engined sports car borne from the platform of the Porsche-designed "people's car", the VW Beetle. It stayed in production for 17 years, but by 1956 Porsche was seeking a successor.

"The plan for the new model was that it should be a comfortable touring car," recalled Mr Ferry Porsche, son of Mr Ferdinand Porsche Senior, the company's founder. "Various models were designed with the aim of creating a true four-seater, but we didn't want the world-famous Porsche shape to disappear."

After rejecting countless concepts from external design houses for the "Type 7" car, Porsche decided it would design the car itself.

The man charged with creating it was Mr Ferry Porsche's son, Mr Ferdinand Alexander Porsche, AKA "Butzi", who was still only in his twenties. The brief given to him by his father was that the new car must retain the Porsche shape, but be reimagined for the 1960s with more space inside, and that it should include "luggage space that could take an owner's golf clubs".

The result, designed with Porsche's body engineer Mr Erwin Komenda, was a model that encompassed a long bonnet, a sloping roofline and a powerful six-cylinder engine. It was simple and beautiful. "Design must be functional, and functionality must be translated into visual aesthetics without any reliance on gimmicks that have to be explained," its creator said.

At the Frankfurt Motor Show in 1963, Porsche unveiled the 901. And if it wasn't for the fact that Peugeot complained about the name – the French manufacturer claimed a patent on three-digit numbers with a zero in the middle – we would probably still be talking about the 50-year longevity of the 901. As it was, Porsche simply swapped the "0" for a "1".

According to a report by the Associated Press at the time: "The new car was mobbed and groped when it was unveiled... show-goers left the doors and roof smeared with fingerprints as they scrambled for a chance to sit behind the wheel." The original price tag for the 911 when it went on sale the following year was $6,500, and the rest is automotive history, with seven generations of the car coming and going over the past half century.

In that time the car evolved – most noticeably in 1998 when it switched from an air-cooled engine to a water-cooled engine – and yet resolutely remained the same, keeping its distinctive shape. It is a dichotomy that appeals to Mr Michael Mauer, the current head of Porsche design and the man behind the latest 911 incarnation.

"There are two things we can play around with," says Mr Mauer. "Firstly, our brand identity. Every car we do is recognisable as a Porsche. We have some very well-identified elements that have helped us establish that. On top of that, each Porsche then has its

911S 2.2 Coupé, 1970

own product identity, which gives us an additional opportunity to play with design cues... For me, the 911 still stands as the embodiment of car design."

Not only is the 911 an iconic car, it has always been beloved by legends. In the late 1960s and early 1970s, Mr Steve McQueen owned three slate-grey 911s, deliberately making them inconspicuous so that he could race around the LA Canyon without attracting too much attention. Mr McQueen even had a switch fitted on his last Porsche (the 911 Carrera Turbo) that cut the rear lights just in case any highway patrolmen were following him. (The 1970 911S Porsche that Mr McQueen drove at the start of the film *Le Mans* was sold for more than £830,000 in 2011.)

Comedian Mr Jerry Seinfeld is another fan, happily describing himself as a "Porschephile". With a collection of more than 40 classic cars, Mr Seinfeld is well placed to explain the success of the German automotive giant: "'Cool' is what sells sports cars. I mean, can you name another company in the history of companies that could get a positive PR spin from [James Dean's death]?"

For Mr Seinfeld, the 911 stands out as the definitive driver's car. "If you ask me, the front of the 911 reminds me of a human face," he said. "Yet I find the location of the speedometer much more significant. This was what impressed me the most when I sat in a Porsche for the first time. This car's priority is speed. Period."

Mr Ferry Porsche, however, speaking shortly before his death in 1998, saw the appeal of one of the most recognisable cars on the planet like this: "The 911 is the only car you could drive on an African safari or at Le Mans, to the theatre or through New York City traffic."

911 Carrera Coupé, Type 991, 2012

THE DAYBREAKERS

*Four business leaders reveal how their success
begins with a morning well spent*

Words by Mr Stephen Armstrong

EVERY AIRPORT is rammed with business books – the self-help manuals for the modern male – all trying to tell you what exactly it is that makes successful men successful, from *The Effective Habits of Highly Effective People* to *Mastering the Rockefeller Habits.* However, when MR PORTER was growing up, Mother Porter always used to say that the most important thing was making a good start to the day – so we decided to monitor the mornings of four leading CEOs and chairmen to see if they offered any clues to how they seize the day.

What did we learn? That CEOs are out of bed by 7.00am. That they love newspapers, hate Twitter and have very specific tastes in radio. That they drink black coffee. That they walk to work more often than most people. That they dress fairly casually. And that, without exception, the first thing they reach for when they open their eyes is their smartphone.

MR ANDREW WILLIAMS
CEO and co-founder of City Financial

Mr Andrew Williams, 41, is chief executive and co-founder of City Financial – one of the UK's fastest-growing independent fund managers. In his time at the head of investment companies in the UK and Canada, Mr Williams acquired a reputation as a cool head in a crisis, and City Financial has grown throughout the downturn.

What time do you usually wake up?
No two days are the same but on a typical morning it's 5.45am. I always set an alarm – I have an old clock radio – but I usually wake up before it goes off. It's feet on the floor within about 10 seconds of consciousness. Frequently, the alarm goes off while I'm in the shower because I've forgotten to turn it off.

What's the first thing you do?
I have a cocker spaniel and she sits very patiently at the bottom of the stairs, so first order of business is always a quick visit. The second stop is always the espresso machine. While I'm doing that I turn on my phone.

Is that when you first check your emails?
Yes. We have business in Asia, so the first thing I do is see if there's anything overnight from them, or any of the sources of information that we get on that market, that is time sensitive. There almost never is. Then I usually go to the gym.

Do you always exercise before breakfast?
The gym's about two minutes away, so I'll just walk over there. It's usually cardiovascular and weights. I've got a great trainer. If I'm not doing that I'll take Poppy [the cocker spaniel] to Kensington Gardens. Then I go back to the house or finish at the gym at 7.30am.

What's your bathroom routine?
Just a shower. If I'm at the gym there's a really excellent café so I'll eat breakfast there.

What's your breakfast preference?
A proper meal such as chicken breast or steak. It's also one of the very few times of day that I'm left alone – between 5.45am and 7.45am people tend not to ring you, so you can safely shut it all off and not delay anything.

What are your morning media habits?

I'll flick through the *Financial Times* – generally speaking I try not to take in too much current information too early in the morning. I think that's a mistake. If you have a good company strategy it should exist for months or years. If you over-bombard yourself with Twitter and Facebook you run the risk of getting pulled and jerked in all sorts of directions. Part of what I try to do in the morning is quite meditative – not getting drawn in to whatever the short-term stuff is.

And then you dress for work?

Yes, I put on my suit. Richard James and Brioni suits are the only ones that I ever wear. Some of my suits have slightly different weights. Richard James does a very good heavy one that doesn't crease and is great for travelling. The Brioni ones are quite delicate. I always have a tie with me; I don't necessarily start the morning with it but I always have it in my pocket in case it needs to go on at some point. My shirts are all organised – my housekeeper puts them in order – whites, pale pink, pale blue, pinstripes, then checks and solid colours. I can basically do it with my eyes closed. Shoes are always from John Lobb – that's 10 years of habit.

How do you get to work?

Breakfast finishes at around 8.30am, and I'm in the office between 9.00am and 10.00am. Our office is in the City. If I need to speak with people on the phone then I'll have a car take me. If I need to read something I'll go on the tube – it's quite quick between Sloane Square and Mansion House, and there's no point in sitting in traffic if you're travelling post-nine o'clock, plus you're not squished like a sardine. It's completely a function of practicality; I don't have the luxury of having a habit, if that makes sense.

MR HANI FARSI
CEO of Corniche Group

Mr Hani Farsi, 46, CEO of Corniche Group, was born in Saudi Arabia and studied in the US. He moved to London in 1993 to set up the Farsi family UK office. In 2007 he established Corniche, which invests in IT, media, film production (Mr Farsi was executive producer of *The Reluctant Fundamentalist*), energy and mineral resources.

What time do you usually wake up?

Usually around 7.00am, sometimes a bit earlier, but that is when my phone alarm goes off. I used to have a clock alarm but the phone means I can check any voice messages or BBMs or emails as soon as I'm awake. I'm dealing with other time zones so I like to see if there are any messages from the Middle East, or somewhere else, waiting for me.

Is that when you send your first email?

If there's anything really urgent or something that is an emergency, I reply; otherwise I'm just looking at the emails to get a glimpse of what the day might look like. I switch on my laptop and scan the headlines. I go straight to the BBC, then various news organisations from the Middle East, then *The Guardian* and *The Telegraph*, just to see if there's anything major that has happened.

What do you do when you get out of bed?

I usually go downstairs to the kitchen and make myself a really healthy vegetable juice – which is something I've been getting into of late.

What are your morning media habits?

I finally cancelled my subscriptions to all my newspapers about two and a half years ago. I used to get a stack of every paper from the extreme right wing to the loony left, to get a complete flavour. But I realised I'd read them about 18 hours ago on the internet. The phone and the laptop have completely replaced that. I switch on the TV news stations and jump between them – although I prefer the BBC as it doesn't waste time with commercials and banter.

Do you do any exercise before breakfast?

Three days a week I go to the gym in the Bulgari Hotel – Bodyism – and train for an hour. If not, I head for the bathroom.

What's your bathroom routine?
I shower, never bath, and obviously I don't shave but I may trim my beard. Then I get dressed.

How do you pick your clothes for the day?
It depends on who I'm meeting. If I'm in my own office, I like to be casual, so it's usually a blazer, jeans and a shirt if the meetings are with a film director or an architect. If it's more on the financial side it's a suit and shirt, no tie. Ready-to-wear will be Kiton, Tom Ford, Loro Piana and Zegna. I get bespoke shirts from Emma Willis and Charvet, and bespoke suits from Huntsman. Shoes – I like Berluti and Lobb. It's the same when I'm in the gym: I take my clothes with me and I change there, have a coffee upstairs and then head straight to the office.

What about breakfast?
No – it's just the vegetable juice. It actually has absolutely everything your body needs. Then a coffee, and if I'm working out then the guys at Bodyism will make me a shake. I'm not a hungry person first thing in the morning.

How do you get to work?
I live in Mayfair and I have for 20 years. Actually I've lived in that house more than I've lived anywhere. It has a lot of history – Errol Flynn used to live there, and before that Douglas Fairbanks. It's about 12 minutes away from my office – it's a nice walk and I choose different routes. I really want to sharpen my senses of observation and see if I'm noticing new things. I use that time for myself – I usually won't be answering the phone. I disconnect just slightly and prepare for the first meetings. It's almost meditative; it's just good sometimes to completely take stock, think, clear your head and mentally and spiritually prepare for the day. Otherwise, I don't feel I accomplish as much in my day.

MR MIKAEL SCHILLER
Executive chairman of Acne Studios

Mr Mikael Schiller, 38, became executive chairman of Acne Studios after 10 years as CEO of the hip Swedish apparel company. Born out of a creative collective in 1996, the company has been expanding across the globe after a restructure into a more conventional business operation put Mr Schiller and co-founder and designer Mr Jonny Johansson at the helm. Acne Studios is now a highly profitable business – $112m in revenue in 2012 alone – stitching ready-to-wear, footwear, accessories and premium denim.

What time do you usually wake up?
Well, two years ago I got an apartment in New York – our head office is in Stockholm and I have a house there, and it's very different in each place. I usually wake up at about 6.00am in Stockholm – earlier in New York.

What's the first thing you do?
I check my emails on my phone. I know I shouldn't – I'd like to get away from that in a way. I don't read them. I just see if there's anything extra interesting.

What do you do when you get out of bed?
When I'm in Sweden I live on an island so quite often I actually start by taking a swim. I might run around the island twice, that's 6km – and then take a swim afterwards. It's not like exercise, it's just to shake me awake.

What are your morning media habits?
I'm quite old school – I still really like newspapers. If I'm travelling and staying in a hotel I usually get the *International Herald Tribune* or the *Financial Times*. I have *The New York Times* on my iPad and I like listening to Swedish radio as well – we have a programme called *Godmorgon, Världen* that's about foreign affairs.

If the swim doesn't count as exercise, do you do any proper exercise?
In Sweden I don't really exercise in the morning – I prefer during the day or before dinner. When I'm in New York I do run in the morning or sometimes I go to yoga. There's an Ashtanga class just across the street. I'm really bad at it, I'm really stiff, but I feel great afterwards.

What's your bathroom routine?
Just a shower. I think people expect fashion people to be very fussy about getting ready but I find it's the opposite. People joke around with me sometimes because they say I look like a bum.

Does that apply when you get dressed?
Yes [laughs]. Sometimes I wear suits, but sometimes I wear a T-shirt and jeans. The weird thing with working in fashion is that you never have to be well dressed. If you work in banking or you're a lawyer you have to be dressed in a certain way to be taken seriously. In the fashion world it's not really like that. I obviously wear a lot of our own clothes, but I like Nike as well, and also very traditional shoes such as Church's.

What about breakfast?
In New York I often go to Balthazar because it's just around the corner and if you're really early it's empty. In Stockholm I go to very old-school places.

So you have breakfast on the way to work?
Yes. I leave maybe at 8.00am – or earlier. In summer in Stockholm I take my boat – it's like a very small speedboat. I have about an eight-minute ride, where I drive myself. I usually stand up in the boat and that's a real moment for me to think and get ready for the day. Then I go by subway or take my bike to the office. Recently I've actually been walking. It's like one and a half hours, but if I've woken up early and I'm not in a hurry then I meet up with a friend for breakfast on the way, and even walk together, which is quite nice. Obviously it's very different in New York, where I live on Crosby Street, and our office is on Broadway. So it's five minutes' walk and I can listen to some podcasts and stuff like that.

MR ARNAUD BAMBERGER
Executive chairman of Cartier UK

Mr Arnaud Bamberger, 69, executive chairman of Cartier UK, has
lived in Britain for 20 years, where he has doubled the turnover
of the company – which is one of the oldest luxury jewellers in
the world. He has been awarded the Ordre des Arts et des Lettres
by the French Minister of Culture and is president of the French
Chamber of Commerce in London.

What time do you usually wake up?
I get up between 7.00am and 7.15am every day. I have a clock, but I only put the alarm on if I have a very important meeting. Otherwise, I wake up by myself.

What's the first thing you do?
I put on the radio and I check my emails – a few emails get me started, such as the figures from the day before, which I always receive at the same time. If the figures are good I'm happy, and if the figures are not good, I start sending emails asking why not.

Does that lead in to your bathroom routine?
Yes. I shave, and then I take a shower. I only take a bath after a day's shooting or if I really want to relax. I take a hot shower, which I'll switch to very cold just to wake me up. I take my time. That's a privileged time in my bathroom on my own, listening to French radio – Europe 1 on my Roberts. I listen to the French news for at least half an hour while I am shaving.

Do you do any exercise before breakfast?
I don't exercise. I'm not fat, but I'm not slim. I'm comfortable about what I eat and what I drink. I love my red wine. I'm a Bordeaux man. Every day I have a nice bottle of red wine. I'm lucky enough to have a good wine cellar, and I drink it, because if I don't drink it, my children will, and I'd rather do it myself.

So you get dressed after the bathroom?
Yes. I'm a quite conservative guy. I either go to work with a suit or a blazer. I'll only wear a blazer if I don't have something important. My tailor is John Kent – I've known him for 20 years, and he's becoming a very good friend. My shirts are made there too, by one of his partners. With ready-to-wear, I either use Ralph Lauren, where everything suits me perfectly and is not a problem, or one of our brands. Socks: I like red socks, purple socks and cashmere

socks. I have a very difficult time with shoes because I have a high instep, but I have a few pairs of Belluccis.

What are your morning media habits?
I have all the French and English newspapers delivered and I read them when I come down to my kitchen for breakfast. Everything from *The Telegraph* and *The Times* to the *Daily Mail* for trash. I try to read as much as I can during breakfast, and if I don't read it all, I keep them for later on during the day.

What's your breakfast preference?
I'm an egg man. Usually it's a boiled egg but from time to time I ask the cook to do something a bit more fancy. And then I have some fruits and a yoghurt and black coffee. If I get up at 7.00am, I'm at breakfast at around 8.00am and then at 8.30am, I leave.

How do you get to work?
I have a driver but most of the time my driver meets me at the door of the office, because I drive to my office. I have a Jaguar as a company car, and a Bentley as a personal car. So I drive one or the other. Then I meet my driver at the office, and he goes and parks the car, because I'm always in a rush.

MR SHINYA KIMURA

The enigmatic motorcycle engineer behind Chabott Engineering
gives us a tour of his Californian workshop

Words by Ms Jodie Harrison

WITH independent custom shops popping up all over the world's
hippest, design-conscious communities, motorcycles are taking
the place of the now ubiquitous track bike in the hearts of hungry
hipsters looking for a cooler fix. Unlike the majority of pretenders
to the scene of customised motorcycle design, however, 52-year-
old Mr Shinya Kimura is humble and focused, continuing his
nearly three decades of dedicated work beyond both the limelight
and flux of trends and impulses – and all despite the fact that his
bikes are owned by the likes of Mr Brad Pitt.

The founder of Zero Engineering, the Japanese bike studio
that jump-started the craze for custom motorcycles back in
1992 with its stripped-back, bare-metal styling, Mr Kimura
began his current practice, Chabott Engineering, in 2006.
"For me a motorcycle is more than art," he says, as he tinkers
with his latest project. "It is something that brings out my
instincts, the wildness and vulnerability in me." With around
a two-year waiting list and a price-on-application format, his
hand-crafted creations certainly have an elitist appeal that
make them dream toys for cash-rich, time-rich types.

Here, Mr Kimura talks us through his methods and design-cues
while giving us a tour of his unique workspace.

How long have you had your LA workshop?
I've been here seven years. Before that we lived in Tokyo, Japan.

Why California?
There was no particular reason for the move. The weather is good and I can ride my motorcycle every day. There's also a wonderful canyon road near here – Azusa Canyon – I like to ride it as often as I can. It looks like the Isle of Man – I must go to the TT one day.

How do you spend your time in the area?
I go to Utah – to Salt Lake from time to time to race. We race on the Bonneville Salt Flats – where many land speed records were recorded. I have a special bike for this. My top speed is 200kph. I raced this bike about two weeks ago so it's a little dirty.

Your motorcycles are celebrated in the press for their unique styling – how long does it take you to complete each bike?
Each takes about six months. I only make two to three bikes a year. I'm currently building one for a customer in Holland and one for a customer in Michigan. I usually just keep the motor and the twin from the original bike and make or source everything else.

If you could only own one motorcycle – any era or engine – what model would it be?
Me? Only one?! This is a tough question. If you insist – a 1970s Ducati 750SS or 450 Desmo, something like that.

How many motorcycles do you currently own?
I have four right now but over the years have owned around 30 or 40.

How would you describe your design aesthetic?
I don't like to be categorised. I like to be flexible. I like to keep moving and changing. I guess I like things stripped back –

"I love this bike. I have been racing on it
for about seven years."

removing anything unnecessary. Truthfully, I cannot really
describe it – I just don't know how to.

How does the design and build process work?
I start by talking for a long time with the clients. I get images from
them – of anything from music to plants to fashion. I don't draw
anything – but I begin to draw the bike in my mind. I then start
tinkling with metals, playing with ideas. I don't know what I'm
going to build until I finish it.

Do customers get to see the design in progress or collaborate at all?
Not really. This is obviously quite difficult for some clients to
understand as it feels like a gamble. But they have a great trust in
me so it seems to work. It's a rare way of working – especially in
custom motorcycle building. Usually people draw something out

and make a computer rendition. For me, if I see it before I build it I get bored of it.

Why do you think there is this new interest in old motorcycles?
Motorcycles these days are almost perfect. They keep getting better and better with very sophisticated technologies within them. But human beings have stayed the same. Getting onto an old motorcycle feels like getting back to basics. I think that's the appeal. It's good to feel metals rather than plastics. You can fall in love with metals as they feel more like a part of nature.

Does your fascination and obsession with mechanical parts extend beyond motorcycles?
Yes. Anything with tyres.

Could you ever envisage doing anything else?
No. I can't. I have no choice.

HOW TO CARRY OFF PYJAMAS

Because dressing well is a full-time occupation

Words by Mr Mansel Fletcher

WE BELIEVE IN the oft-repeated aphorism, "A gentleman uses a butter knife even when dining alone." However, this isn't about *Downton Abbey* pretensions, or *Brideshead Revisited* fantasies, it's about living elegantly, and by extension dressing elegantly, wherever you are. Why let standards slip when you're on home turf?

That said, we're the first to recognise that comfort is a priority at the end of the day, and the more formal a man's working wardrobe the more important it will be for him to kick off his John Lobb shoes, hang up his Richard James suit and toss his Charvet shirt into the laundry basket when he gets home. The logic of this, however, isn't to then dress like a bum in an old pair of NBA replica shorts and a greying wife-beater, but instead to seek out elegant loungewear. At its best this takes the form of a pair of pyjamas and a dressing gown, a combination as comfortable as a sweat suit, but as elegant as a good suit.

If you're still unconvinced of the need to dress up at home it's relevant to mention that, aside from delivery drivers and neighbours, the people who see you in your loungewear are the people whose opinions really count – wives, girlfriends, partners and children. Of course it's true that no man is a hero to his valet (as Monsieur Michel de Montaigne observed in the 16th century), but that's a reason to try harder in the company of your nearest and dearest, rather than relax into the sartorial depravity of faded old sweatpants. Just ask yourself if you'd like your girlfriend to start dressing in cut-off joggers and an old vest.

Like every other piece of clothing, pyjamas make a statement. They speak of a more civilised age, when men had time to read a newspaper while they ate breakfast, and enjoy a quiet glass of whisky before bed. They also tell a tale of much draughtier bedrooms than we're used to, and hark back to the (now unthinkable) days when gentlemen didn't work; the era of Mr PG Wodehouse's fictional character Bertie Wooster, who rarely rose before 9am, and is said, in 1934's *Thank You, Jeeves*, to wear heliotrope-coloured pyjamas. For good or bad those days have gone, and they aren't coming back. However, they still have a lot to teach us about style, elegance and doing things well, even if it's sometimes hard to achieve these things while having to simultaneously earn a living.

Perhaps it's telling that Wooster was unlucky in love, because whatever men did in the 1930s these days there is one domestic situation for which pyjamas are ill-suited. If, after a date, a guy is entertaining a girl in his bedroom, especially if it's the first time he's entertained this particular girl, then pyjamas might not strike the right note – she shouldn't be given reason to wonder if he's more used to sleeping with teddy bears than with women. The truth is that pyjamas' easy cut, and the fact that they cover the entire body, means that they're more sophisticated than seductive. On such occasions classic white cotton boxer shorts are probably the best option.

Assuming the white boxers are well received, and more dates follow, then after the initial frenzy of love has relaxed into something more dependable, a man may revert to wearing pyjamas. They announce that he's a man of style, both in public and in private. Complete the outfit with a proper dressing gown (keep the towelling bathrobe for the bathroom), and a pair of velvet slippers. And if you do get to wake up in time to enjoy breakfast in your splendid new nightwear then do remember to use a butter knife when you prepare your toast or croissant.

Mr Thomas Beck in a studio portrait, circa 1935

MR DOMINIC COOPER

The actor mentions spies, Bond and clothes as an oh-so-subtle hint about his own 007 aspirations

Words by Mr Chris Elvidge

"EVERY MAN DREAMS of playing 007, right?" At the photographer's request, Mr Dominic Cooper fixes the camera with an expression of effortless suave: equal parts Sir Sean Connery and Sir Roger Moore, with a little "blue steel" thrown in for good measure. The man who would be Bond appears to have nailed the look, at least.

With Mr Daniel Craig set to return for at least one more instalment of the august spy franchise, it looks as if the star of *The History Boys* and *Mamma Mia!* will have to wait a while for the opportunity – but it's unlikely that he'll be too concerned. With a starring role in *Fleming: The Man Who Would be Bond*, a four-part series based on the life of the James Bond creator, he may just have landed the next best thing.

"The story of Fleming has been told before, but never quite like this," says Mr Cooper, back in casual clothes after the shoot. "It's creative, it's exhilarating... it's a reflection, I think, of the kind of person that he wanted to be seen as." So James Bond, in other words? Mr Fleming was an intelligence officer with The Admiralty in London before he was an author, after all, and it's often been said that many of the fictional spy's characteristics, from his love of gambling and cigars to his famously rampant libido, were inspired by the author's own. "Well, Bond was his fantasy, wasn't he?" Mr Cooper admits. "He was his Tyler Durden, the amped-up version of him, and the show certainly acknowledges that. So while the series is rooted in Fleming's life story, creatively, at least, it pays homage to Bond." So it's liberal with the truth, then? "Well, we never set out to tell the absolute truth," he replies, a wry smile spreading across his lips. "I look nothing like him, for a start."

"I loved *The Devil's Double*," he says, while discussing a few of his more adventurous roles. In the film, he played both the eldest son of Saddam Hussein, Uday, and his body double. "When you're playing a real-life character, people often have a very specific idea of that person, and there will always be critics who expect you to give a certain type of performance. But this was just the opposite. I was really encouraged to be daring as an actor. Plus, it's always preferable shooting on these smaller productions. You're allowed to trust in your acting instincts a little more," he says, contrasting it with the large-scale production of *Warcraft*, or 2012's preposterous – but surprisingly enjoyable – *Abraham Lincoln: Vampire Hunter*.

Having trained in film editing prior to embarking on his acting career, it makes perfect sense that Mr Cooper should feel drawn to the creative side of his craft, and he admits to harbouring ambitions behind the lens – but not quite yet. "I've always loved photography," he says, "and I really admire what directors do. I find myself picking up a lot when I'm on set, too. But it's about finding something that's inspiring to you. It's got to be the right project at the right time. I'm very excited to reach that point, where I'm ready to give it a go."

Could that be something to do if the James Bond gig falls through, then?

"Well, it's always good to have a plan B, isn't it?"

STARS IN THEIR CARS

These guys knew how to hit the road in style…

Words by Mr Mansel Fletcher

THERE IS MORE to being well dressed than just the clothes. It's about the life as well as the wardrobe, and a man's method of transport is an important element of the stylish life. If you're offering someone a lift home after dinner it's more tempting if she knows that you've got the keys to an Aston in your pocket, rather than the keys to a D-lock. This is something the men featured here knew well, and they set an almost unbeatable benchmark when it comes to automotive style.

FORD THUNDERBIRD (PREVIOUS PAGE)
Mr Arthur Miller

Looking at this 1956 photograph of Mr Arthur Miller nonchalantly driving his Ford Thunderbird in Connecticut, with his wife Ms Marilyn Monroe in the passenger seat, it's hard to remember that he was a playwright, rather than a playboy. There's little about his car's extravagant lines, or his wife's curves, that you'd associate with a bookish personality. The only clues are his wool sweater and casual shirt.

FERRARI 250 GT LUSSO
Mr James Coburn

Mr James Coburn, a Hollywood tough guy who appeared in Mr Sean Peckinpah's classic 1977 film *Cross of Iron*, is often remembered more for the cars he drove than his films. He owned a 250 GT California, a car that British radio DJ Chris Evans bought for more than £5m in 2008, as well as this beautiful V12 Lusso, pictured at his Los Angeles home in 1966, which was designed by Italian coach-builder Pininfarina.

CADILLAC ELDORADO
Mr Richard Burton

When Mr Richard Burton met Dame Elizabeth Taylor on the set of the 1963 film *Cleopatra* he reportedly declared that he'd sleep with her within 48 hours. In the end it's said that five days passed before they consummated their relationship. And the reason we're rehearsing this gossip? They are said to have first made love together on the back seat of Mr Burton's Cadillac, seen here in this photograph taken circa 1955.

TRIUMPH TR3
Mr Johnny Hallyday

The appeal of most French exports, things such as red Bordeaux wine, the classic Citroën DS and Ms Laetitia Casta, is apparent. The appeal of singer Mr Johnny Hallyday, however, remains a mystery beyond his country's borders, but that detracts nothing from his appearance in a soft-shouldered jacket behind the wheel of a TR3, with Paris' Arc de Triomphe in the background, in 1965.

JAGUAR E-TYPE
Mr Dean Martin

Mr Frank Sinatra was the best-dressed member of the Rat Pack, but Mr Dean Martin (*bottom left*), pictured arriving at NBC Studios in California circa 1968, clearly had better taste in cars – Ol' Blue Eyes' last motor was a Chrysler LeBaron station wagon. Jaguar's famous E-Type is arguably the most beautiful of the 1960s sports cars, but unlike most it's relatively affordable today.

JAGUAR XKSS
Mr Steve McQueen

Mr Steve McQueen was interested in guy stuff – he's also said to have turned down a date with Ms Ali MacGraw in order to wax his Belstaff jacket. While most closely associated with the Ford Mustang he drove in *Bullitt,* he chose to drive a Jaguar XKSS, pictured here in 1963, to Hollywood's studios. The car is a bizarrely proportioned, road-going version of the Le Mans-winning D-Type.

FERRARI 250 GT
Mr Jean-Paul Belmondo

It's hard to think that any man, regardless of his clothes, could look bad in a 250 GT, but it's just as hard to think of how a man could look cooler at the wheel than French actor Mr Jean-Paul Belmondo does, dressed in a suit and tie. Note that not even this icon of France's legendary, *ennui*-filled New Wave cinema can resist grinning like the Cheshire cat as he speeds along in a 250 GT in this photo taken in France in 1962.

THE DEATH OF THE BEARD

Why the buzz for facial fuzz has finally reached its peak…

Words by Mr Mansel Fletcher

AT ITS BEST a full beard, worn in the fashion of the notorious Australian outdoorsman Mr Ned Kelly, makes a man look distinguished. Which begs the enquiry, "What happens when everyone's got a beard?" That was the question that a team from Australia's University of New South Wales set out to answer, and their unsurprising conclusion is that the appeal of beards diminishes in line with their popularity. Yet early in 2014 the *New York Post* broke the news that men are becoming so desperate to grow a beard that increasing numbers are having plastic surgery to remove hair follicles from their scalp and have them plugged into their face. No wonder there's often a self-consciousness about beards that's incompatible with their supposed air of authenticity.

For these reasons, among others, here at MR PORTER we're beginning to ask if time's up for beards, because they're now boringly ubiquitous and their cultural *raison d'être* is becoming absurd. An example of the latter: an email pinged in my inbox recently. It was from a New York vendor of designer outdoor gear and was promoting some of that vendor's upcoming customer events. These workshops include "axe restoration", "heart of sourdough" and "knife sharpening". The same weekend I saw a new spring catalogue from a very middle-of-the-road British mail-order clothing company featuring a male model with a thin beard. And as an aside, once neo-Luddite hipsters are sharpening axes in a way that would excite fictional yuppie antihero Patrick Bateman, aren't these hitherto separate worlds of men's style collapsing in on themselves?

But let's be fair to the hipster *zeitgeist*, because while it's easy to mock the urban lumberjack, any man who spends his cosseted days in an air-conditioned office, operating an Apple computer with an ultra-fast internet connection, and a world of gourmet lunch options five minutes from his desk, can be forgiven for fantasising about the romance of real work. For dreaming of the deep satisfaction that would come from an honest day's toil in the great outdoors, chopping wood, corralling cattle, or tilling the land, and for imagining, as he queues outside the latest burger restaurant, that one day he might hunt his own food and sleep under the stars. This is the mood that has informed the trend for beards, and which combines with an understandable wish to accentuate one's masculinity in a world where it's not always clear how to positively interpret being a man. It's no coincidence that the last grooming trend was the unsavoury and emasculating craze for extreme waxing and shaving.

But what if, rather than revealing our connection with "real life", this Luddite urge reveals our disconnection from it? How far does the *zeitgeist*'s art-directed vision of the demanding, exhausting and potentially dangerous world of physical labour actually tally with reality? If we really want to emulate the style of our manually labouring forebears then we'll take every opportunity to wear and enjoy the clothes that preclude the possibility of physical work, rather than dressing down in the hope that someone will mistake us for a blacksmith. It's all very well spending a weekend building your own barbecue, but I want to speak up for the guys who are more interested in putting on a blazer and heading out to a restaurant where they can enjoy food cooked by someone else.

And where does fashion come into all this? Five or six years ago, when the current neo-dandy trend was new and fresh, old-fashioned beards were rare and correspondingly interesting. Now they're in danger of alternating between replacing the bow tie (and they're frequently worn by guys in bow ties) as a crude signifier of a simplistic interest in style, and as an absurd statement of intent on behalf of hipsters whose Victorian pimp-inspired grooming is at odds with their contemporary lifestyle. Let's stop this now, before there's a revival of Victorian mutton-chop sideburns, and before we forget that sporting such antiquated facial topiary will probably make you the subject of a lot of laughter.

While shaving off a beard that's been carefully nurtured over the course of four months is not a decision to be taken lightly, a brief review of suave, fresh-faced icons past and present – men such as Messrs Cary Grant, Gary Cooper, Richard Gere and Mark Ronson – makes a pretty convincing case for going smooth. Now, where did we put that razor?

MR NICKY DUNNE

*The chairman of celebrated bookshop Heywood Hill
tells us what makes the Mayfair store so relevant*

Words by Mr Mansel Fletcher

THE FIRST EXISTENTIAL THREAT to face Mayfair's Heywood Hill bookshop came in the form of the blitz of WWII, when the Nazis' bombs poured down onto London. It was a threat with which the founder, Mr George Heywood Hill, was well acquainted as he was away fighting in the war, having been called up in 1942. He employed the famous author Ms Nancy Mitford to run the shop in his absence, and she, in the words of today's chairman Mr Nicky Dunne, "Put the place on the map. She had a magnetic personality, by which I mean she had the ability to attract as well as repel, but she attracted more than she repelled."

However, in the past decade the shop has faced a different, but equally grave threat: the digitisation of the buying, and reading, of books. This is the challenge that has faced Mr Dunne since he took charge of the shop in June 2011. Prior to that, the shop "was run without much of a sense that it needed to do very much," according to Mr Dunne. His words, and his enthusiasm, make it clear that he takes a very different view, and he's building a future for Heywood Hill on three different kinds of activity.

"On the antiquarian side it's about finding the collectors among our customers and doing some work for them," he says. "We recently bought a first, English edition of James Joyce's *Ulysses*, with the Eric Gill cover. The second thing we do is to create private libraries. That could be for someone who wants to give their husband 50 books on fishing, or it could be a large-scale private library – we recently finished one in Switzerland on different aspects of modernism, rooted in interwar German expressionism. The third thing we do is subscription services, where we choose books for people, either for themselves or as gifts. Every month I sit down and think of four books to send to a customer in the Hamptons, and we take a lot of care over it."

It's hard to resist the temptation to describe this last service as the aristocratic Amazon, and in many ways Heywood Hill's personal, old-world service is the antithesis of the online retailer. Mr Dunne gives an extreme example: "The other day an American customer wanted to give a book to someone and the only opportunity we had to get it to him was in the arrivals hall at Gatwick Airport. So one of us went down there to hand it over – we will go to a very far degree to do whatever our customers want."

The private library focuses on 20th-century books
in English on Arabia and Islam

FAIRWAYS TO HEAVEN

*Eight breathtaking golf courses guaranteed to deliver
drama in both scene and swing*

Words by Mr Dan Davies

GOLF is unlike any other sport in that no two playing arenas
are even remotely alike. From the humps, bumps and hollows
of the historic links courses bordering the sea – terrain that has
been largely fashioned by nature – to the tree-lined, manicured
acres of park and heathland courses where the ground has been
landscaped and sculpted to the architect's specifications, this is
a sport in which the venues receive equal billing with the game's
very best players. Better still, most of these courses are accessible
to anyone with an official club handicap – and an appropriately
healthy bank balance. So, here are eight places you really must play
before you die.

OLD COURSE, ST ANDREWS
Scotland

The "home of golf" is a course like no other. Contained within
a strip of land in the shape of a shepherd's crook, it plays out to
a loop at the turn and then back towards the historic university
town, where the 18th green, scene of so many of the sport's
defining moments, nestles beneath the sentinel of the Royal and
Ancient Golf Club. A Mecca for golfing pilgrims, the Old Course

has evolved over the 600 years golf has been played here. And while some remain critical of its myriad unique features – massive double greens, cavernous bunkers and shared fairways between holes – the proof is in those who laud it above all others, all-time greats Messrs Bobby Jones and Tiger Woods to name but two.

PINE VALLEY
US

Regularly ranked as the No.1 course in the US, Pine Valley (*above*) was set up in 1912 by a Philadelphian golfing group. It has never hosted a professional event, chiefly because its designer, Mr George Crump, felt that no fairway should be visible from any other, meaning there isn't the space to take spectators. It is considered to have the finest collection of par-3s, par-4s and par-5s on the planet, as well as the best start and the best finish: in other words, there are no weaknesses. Its natural splendour and the demands it places on golfers have attracted the game's finest, many of whom have left their own mark on this slice of golfing heaven.

WEST COURSE, ROYAL MELBOURNE
Australia

With huge greens, invitingly wide fairways and a total lack of water hazards, the West Course at Royal Melbourne doesn't, on paper, sound like a challenge. But Dr Alister MacKenzie, the Scot who designed the Augusta National, knew what he was doing when in 1926 he saw this expanse of sand belt in the Black Rock suburb of the city. And in Mr Mick Morcom, a greenkeeper he described as the best he ever worked with, he found the man to realise his vision. Strategy is the key to a good score here; principles Mr MacKenzie absorbed from his years studying the Old Course at St Andrews.

ROYAL COUNTY DOWN
Northern Ireland

Designed in 1889, this beautiful links (*above*) near Newcastle is a fixture for golfers everywhere. Framed by the mountains of Mourne, the Irish Sea and towering dunes, its quirky layout features several blind tee shots and hard, fast-running fairways.

But it's the beauty of the surroundings, the quality of the turf and the enduring genius of its test – the first nine holes have been described by five-time British Open Champion Mr Tom Watson as the best he has ever played – that mark it out as a true classic.

PACIFIC DUNES
US

Golf began on the rough ground – the links – between farmland and the beach, and Pacific Dunes (*above*), the pick of the courses at Bandon Dunes Golf Resort, looks as if it has been in play for hundreds of years. But although its natural beauty and rugged terrain resemble the very best of the historic links courses of Scotland, England and Ireland, this is a modern masterpiece courtesy of Mr Tom Doak. The course begins amid 60ft sea pines before emerging into a stretch of the South Oregon real estate that looks as if God bequeathed it to the game. Firm fairways and tight lies remain true to the links tradition, and the holes hugging the coast are among the most spectacular in world golf.

SUNNINGDALE
England

Boasting two championship courses and bucolic views of the Berkshire countryside, Sunningdale is one of the great pleasures in a golfer's life – particularly if you spend a summer day enjoying both the Old and New courses. This is classic heathland fare, laid out on sandy terrain that drains well and offers perfect turf from which to clip crisp iron shots or float delicate chips. The Old Course, with its towering trees, banks of heather and wispy brown rough, is a delight, while the New Course represents arguably the tougher examination.

CAPE KIDNAPPERS
New Zealand

It's hard to imagine a more dramatic setting for a course than the one Mr Tom Doak – yes, him again – has manicured on the tip of Hawke's Bay on the east coast of the North Island (*above*). One of the wonders of modern golf, his 7,119-yard layout resembles something from a fantasy golf calendar in which holes are hewn from mountainsides or played to island greens. At Cape Kidnappers, however, the hazards are all too real: undulating greens and rippling fairways flanked by deep ravines. A shot offline will not merely disappear into vegetation; it will take an age falling to its final resting place in the Pacific Ocean – if nothing else, making for the most memorable mishit in golf.

CLUB DE GOLF VALDERRAMA
Spain

Valderrama (*above*), on Spain's southern tip, began life in 1974 under a different name: Las Aves. In 1985, Mr Jaime Ortiz Patiño, the grandson of a Bolivian billionaire, transformed it into the jewel in the crown of European golf. It was totally redesigned by its original architect, Mr Robert Trent Jones, garnering a reputation for being one of the sternest tests in the game, and also for its immaculate presentation. Tight fairways that wind between cork oak trees, lightning-fast greens and epic holes such as the par-5 fourth, with its two-tiered green guarded by a lake with waterfalls, have challenged the best in both the Volvo Masters and the 1997 Ryder Cup, the first played on mainland Europe.

ON THE SLOPES

How to look the part, whether on or off the mountain

Words by Mr Mansel Fletcher

IN THE MOUNTAINS it's reasonable to prioritise Fahrenheit over fashion. However, there's no reason why, with the right clothes, a man can't stay warm on the inside and look cool on the outside. It takes a moment to remember what works in the snow, in terms of colours and textures, as well as in terms of comfort, warmth and style. Even men who stick to dark hues for city life should consider extending the colour palette when packing for a week on the slopes.

Although we firmly stand by all the advice given below, we also retain an admiration for the British actor Mr Bill Nighy, who once told MR PORTER that he went to Chamonix, a French ski resort, wearing a navy two-piece suit, a Crombie coat and a trilby.

THE EIGHT RULES OF
MOUNTAIN STYLE

I

Skiing, like any other sport, can be a sweaty business. Pack a fresh base layer, and fresh socks, for every day of the holiday. Also, a man who wants to put on dry gloves each morning will need to take two pairs.

2

The days when grand Swiss hotels demanded that their male guests wear a dinner jacket in the dining room may have gone, but that doesn't mean that standards have entirely slipped. Consider packing a jacket, a half-zip cashmere sweater and a knitted tie if you plan to eat in the best restaurants.

3

The rollneck really comes into its own on the piste, giving you much-needed protection against the wind at all times, and preventing the dreaded scenario of snow going down your shirt in the event of a major wipeout.

4

If it's business as usual, even up the mountain, then look out for Kjus' Bluetooth gloves, which contain a speaker and microphone and will allow you to take calls without fumbling in your pockets.

5

The right pair of sunglasses are vital if a man's to avoid snow blindness, but we'd also consider taking a pair of goggles in order to better handle the range of possible weather conditions.

6

Don't forget to take a well-stocked sponge bag because grooming is a necessity rather than an indulgence. You need sun block for the face, neck, ears and lips, nourishing moisturiser to put on at night, as well as the usual shower gel, shampoo, lip balm and aftershave.

7

Snow-strewn streets call for serious footwear – rubber-soled leather boots are the obvious choice because they'll stay dry and afford you some grip. If you can find fur-lined ones, so much the better.

8

Take a light pair of house shoes or slippers to wear around the chalet, to avoid the unhappy experience of stepping in snowmelt after you've taken your ski boots off.

Mr Gianni Agnelli, Italy, 1967

L'Avvocato didn't let a leg injury stop him skiing, and here he is seen with a brace over his trousers. He also wears a rollneck and overshirt and looks as if he knows exactly what he's doing on the piste.

Mr Robert Redford, US, 1969

Sporting an enviable moustache, Mr Redford contemplates what
appears to be a vertiginous slope, and a spectacular view. He
wears very slim black trousers, a short black jacket, a rollneck and
a well-proportioned woolly hat. Any hipsters planning to go skiing
would do well to follow Mr Redford's example.

HRH Prince Charles, Switzerland, 1981

HRH Prince Charles, captured here in his younger days, keeps out
the wind with an azure rollneck the colour of the sky, and a checked
neckerchief that complements the blue. He also wears a dark blue
ski suit and an appropriately rugged-looking military watch on
a nylon Nato strap. He makes a stylish, yet purposeful, impression.

Ms Nathalie and Mr Alain Delon, Switzerland, 1967

The French style icon wears a rather insubstantial-looking padded anorak in Verbier, and, perhaps for warmth, holds on to his (now ex) wife, Ms Nathalie Delon. He's wearing the slim trousers that were once *de rigueur* on the slopes, and has swapped *Le Samouraï*'s famous fedora for a bobble hat.

Mr Rudolf Matt, Austria, 1932

The Austrian skier, who became the slalom world champion in 1936, looks more like he's dressed for the pub than for a ski race. His oversized tweed cap sits well with his thick sweater, and the buttoned-up white shirt looks modern. His swarthy complexion suggests he didn't much bother about sunscreen.

MR RAY WINSTONE

One of Britain's best-loved character actors and star of biblical epic,
Noah, *on his path from Hackney to Hollywood*

Words by Mr Alex Bilmes, editor-in-chief of British *Esquire*

MR RAY WINSTONE is not an especially religious man – "Family's my religion," he says – but he does believe in luck. It's luck, he says, that got him his first job as an actor. It's luck that led him to Elaine, his wife of more than three decades. Luck that took him from hard-knock east London to a Hollywood movie career. "I'm a very lucky boy," he says, draining his soup as we dine at London's Dean Street Townhouse. Although luck alone can't explain everything: his success is also the result of talent, drive and dedication. "You work hard, sure," he says. "You don't get nothing for nothing."

Mr Winstone, at 57, is the British screen hardman who is also one of his nation's most effective and beloved character actors – not that he likes such a description. Mr Winstone is a big man with a fearful growl, but there's a delicacy to his performances that's remarked upon less often than the sturdy bulk, the manly squint, the thickly gravelled voice and the distinctive London accent.

Dapper, almost dandyish in a three-piece suit over a floral shirt, plus prescription Persol sunglasses (he's mislaid his regular spectacles and apologises profusely for wearing his shades inside), Mr Winstone has been telling me his life story, which is how we got on to the idea of fate, and luck. He's also been filling me in on his film *Noah*, which is how we got on to religion. *Noah* is the director

65

Mr Darren Aronofsky's apocalyptic environmentalist spectacular in which Mr Russell Crowe, as the biblical boat builder, receives instructions from the Creator that a great flood is coming. He assembles an ark to save the world's animals – and his own family – from drowning. Mr Winstone plays Tubal-cain, Noah's nemesis, who believes that the beasts and their environment should be sacrificed to save humanity, rather than the other way around.

Speculation whirlpooled around the film. Mr Aronofsky is a brilliant director of intense, disquieting movies – *Requiem for a Dream, The Wrestler, Black Swan* – but he had never before worked with a budget this large on a production this complicated. Reports tell of difficult shooting conditions, disputes between director and studio, and frayed nerves over the film's potential to excite controversy among religious groups.

"Darren stood his ground and made his film, the film he wanted to make," says Mr Winstone. "It's an emotional journey, an epic. There's nothing in there that's offensive. I'm very proud of it. And you can't say that about every film you do." Pause, wolfish grin. "Even though you have to."

From the beginning of his acting career, Mr Winstone has often played the bad guy. But he doesn't necessarily see them that way, certainly not in the case of his character in *Noah*. Tubal-cain is a hard man, a warrior, but he's not some thoughtless thug. He and Noah are descended from the same kingly bloodline and Mr Winstone plays him as Yin to Mr Crowe's Yang. "I watched a lot of what Russell was doing, trying to get similarities," says Mr Winstone. "I didn't want to play him as the baddie. He's a man with an opinion. But he's also a man who's been shunned by the Creator, and that's turned him to the dark side. So there was a lot in there for me to work with, instead of just playing a one-dimensional bad guy."

Mr Winstone is, to use the parlance, a bit of a ledge. In 1977 he played the terrifying Carlin in *Scum*, the late Mr Alan Clarke's short, sharp, shock of a film, set in a prison for young offenders.

Carlin's famous line, "I'm the daddy now," spat out after a moment of decisive ultra-violence, was echoed with relish by playground ruffians through the 1980s and beyond.

Scum was made as a TV movie for the BBC, which refused to show it, and then subsequently remade – Mr Winstone played Carlin again – for a theatrical release in 1979. In both versions Mr Winstone's performance is so naturalistic it seems he is hardly acting at all. But then it always does. That's his great skill.

"People say [of his characters], 'That's you, isn't it?' You think so? Oh, good! I'm glad you think it's me. But it ain't me. Sometimes it's close to me. But it's not me."

This authenticity is the result of nature and nurture: talent and application, and also the fact that Mr Winstone really does know something about men from tough backgrounds. He was born in inner-city Hackney in 1957 and he grew up first in Plaistow, in the East End, and later on a council estate in Enfield, a resolutely working-class district of north London, where his dad, Raymond Sr, ran a greengrocer business.

He describes his childhood in 1960s London as "fabulous". He recalls long hot summers playing on WWII bombsites. "I remember doors being open. My mum used to make dinner for the old girl over the road. Sunday mornings waking up to Judy Garland, Frank Sinatra. Then you get dressed and go and visit Nan and Grandad. Always put something smart on on a Sunday. That's an East End thing: fur coat and no knickers. It was good times."

In some ways, for all his success, he's never really left east London. He and Elaine live in nearby Essex, traditional escape route for East Enders made good. And Mr Winstone is a committed supporter of West Ham United, the cockney football team of choice.

Mr Winstone was some distance from top of the class at school. "I wasn't an intellectual or anywhere near it," he says. He couldn't read properly until he was 12. He learnt faster at the famous Repton Amateur Boxing Club in Bethnal Green. He was three-time London schoolboy champion at welterweight and he fought twice for England. "I learnt more about how you conduct yourself in the world from boxing than from anything else. Treat people how you wish to be treated. Show respect. Give people a chance."

Acting came later: "There was a girl I fancied who went in the school play so I thought I'll go in. I had no interest whatsoever other than that." He enjoyed it, was passably good at it, and his parents saw acting as something that would keep him out of trouble.

He went to a drama school in London: "Great parties, great girls, I had a ball," he says. But the unfinished working-class lad didn't quite fit in. "They looked at me as a bit of a threat with the accent and all that." After a series of petty infringements, he was expelled. The same day he was thrown out, a group of his fellow students were going for an audition for a TV movie. He wouldn't have joined them otherwise but he tagged along so he could get

them together afterwards to say a final goodbye: "I was hanging around, talking to this receptionist who asked me if I would like to go in and meet the director. She was a good-looking girl so I thought I'd impress her, and I got the part." The movie was *Scum*.

"It's just fate, it's luck," he says. "If I hadn't been expelled, if I hadn't gone with the boys to have a drink with them when I was leaving, if I hadn't have said yes I'd go in and meet him, then I wouldn't be here today. And God knows what I'd have been doing. No idea. I can't see from that point onwards."

The same producers offered him a part in a teen drama called *That Summer!* "That's how I met my wife. Fate, again." They married in 1979, and have three daughters.

By no means did *Scum* and *That Summer!* immediately lead to a Hollywood career. Mr Winstone was paid £1,800 for each, and went on to work mostly in generic British TV.

"Acting was just a giggle to me," he says. "A ridiculous way to get a living. I wasn't very good either. I wasn't disciplined. It was only later I started to take it seriously, when I done *Nil by Mouth*."

Written and directed by Mr Gary Oldman, *Nil by Mouth* is an unflinching family drama, in which Mr Winstone plays Ray, a violent, self-pitying alcoholic based on Mr Oldman's father. Mr Oldman, he says, was "a really good teacher. Best director I've worked with." Mr Winstone's performance was widely acclaimed.

Around the same time he worked at the tiny Royal Court theatre in London with the influential stage director Mr Ian Rickson. "He got rid of my inhibitions, my moods," Mr Winstone says. "I had attitude, without a doubt," he says. "I felt like I wasn't accepted, it was all that inverted snobbery shit. F***ing rubbish."

He still feels it sometimes, the old London resentment boiling up. "You can't get rid of it all," he says. "It's in you."

Two years after *Nil by Mouth*, another British actor turned director, Mr Tim Roth, cast Mr Winstone as an incestuous father in the remorselessly bleak *The War Zone* – further evidence that Mr Winstone was far more than some brutish screen tough.

Then came his most celebrated role, in Mr Jonathan Glazer's devilish *Sexy Beast*, as the safecracker Gal Dove, retired to Spain only to find himself tormented by Sir Ben Kingsley's psychopath, Don. After that Mr Winstone was away, mixing roles in credible indies (*Last Orders, Sex & Drugs & Rock & Roll, The Proposition*) with Hollywood blockbusters (*King Arthur, Beowulf, Indiana Jones and the Kingdom of the Crystal Skull*). He was a favourite of the late Mr Anthony Minghella, who cast him in *Cold Mountain* and *Breaking and Entering*, and of Mr Martin Scorsese, for whom he worked on *The Departed* and *Hugo*. On TV he's been Henry VIII, and Magwitch in *Great Expectations*.

Even now, though, with all that affirmation, he still struggles to accept his fate. "I've never felt like an actor," he says. "I've never felt like I'm in the right game. I look at the sparks [the on-set electricians] and feel like I should have been one of them. I'm one of the boys. A thespian? It don't sit right with me. I feel like a schizophrenic transvestite, you know? I'm a split personality dressing up in other people's clothes."

He gives me an example of the preposterous nature of his existence, from his experience playing Magwitch: "I'm half-naked, I've got chains around me leg, I've all me hair shaved off and me eyebrows, and I'm in the sea just off Essex in December, covered in mud and shit. And you go, 'What am I doing? Raymond, you're 56 years of age, boy! Stop playing!'

"Look," he says, "I'm jesting with you because I love what I'm doing and it's great fun. Just sometimes I sit there and think, 'What am I all about?'"

Whatever he is about, the film industry clearly likes it. Next we will see him as a former mercenary in espionage drama, *The Gunman*, starring Messrs Sean Penn and Javier Bardem.

But before that, he's off to Sicily, with Elaine. His life sounds pretty good to me. "Everything at the moment," he concedes, "is sweet. Touch wood." And he knocks on the table. For luck.

STYLE ICONS

Eighteen men whose dress sense we admire

MR DENNIS HOPPER

The actor and photographer appeared in and sometimes directed the films that defined the 1950s, 1960s, 1970s and 1980s. As you'd expect from a man who featured in *Rebel Without a Cause*, *Easy Rider*, *Apocalypse Now* and *Blue Velvet*, Mr Dennis Hopper was keenly aware of the importance of creating the right look, whether with the perfect olive jacket or a great convertible.

MR LEROY "SATCHEL" PAIGE

What does it say about the elegance of the 1930s that baseball player Mr Satchel Paige looks more like a jazz musician than an athlete? The pointed collar and the loosely cut sleeves show that Mr Paige was a follower of fashion, but his style has endured even longer than his 40-year career as a pitcher. He was famously cocky and charismatic – qualities his outfit eloquently projects. A man's clothes should tell his story, and be relatively honest about it.

MR WALTER BONATTI

These days Italian style breaks down into two parts – flashy designer chic or the elaborately tailored look of the Pitti peacocks. So this 1964 image of explorer Mr Walter Bonatti, who made the first wintertime solo climb of the north face of the Matterhorn, is a revelation. His appearance is refreshingly simple. He was also a romantic and a purist in his approach to mountaineering, which he defined as "victory over your own human frailty".

MR WARREN BEATTY

The Hollywood actor and director has combined a commercially and artistically successful film career with five decades of political activism and, until his 1992 marriage to actress Ms Annette Bening, a reputation as a prolific lover. Whether long-haired in a denim jacket or, as here, clean-cut in a sports jacket, he's always known how to dress with relaxed sophistication.

MR HOWARD HUGHES

Fearless and pioneering aviator, engineer of genius, film producer
and lover of Mses Katharine Hepburn, Bette Davis, Ava Gardner
and Ginger Rogers, among others – for a while Mr Howard
Hughes had it all. To top it off he possessed an excellent sense of
style, and looked as suave in softly tailored jackets and suits as he
did purposeful in leather flying jackets and fedora hats.

MR JOHNNY CARSON

The idea that a chat show host could offer sartorial inspiration seems outlandish in 2014, but US television legend Mr Johnny Carson knew how to dress, and he showed it over the 30 years he anchored *The Tonight Show*. Nearly half a century after he made a habit of wearing odd jackets with dark trousers, it once again looks very relevant.

THE KENNEDY BROTHERS

Their style legacy may not be as important as their political legacy, but President John F Kennedy, Senator Robert F Kennedy and Senator Edward Kennedy remain the poster boys for sophisticated East Coast Ivy League style. Their soft-shouldered suits are an inspiration for office wear, their tweed jackets are perfect weekend wear, and their swim shorts set the pace for beachwear.

MR VITTORIO DE SICA

Born in Lazio, Mr Vittorio De Sica grew up poor in Naples and is a poster boy for the city's distinctive tailoring. Although best known for the neorealism of films such as *Bicycle Thieves*, he dressed in suits cut for him by Mr Vincenzo Attolini, tailor at Mr Gennaro Rubinacci's shop London House. While his clothes were faultlessly formal, they also ensured that he looked at ease – a combination that remains powerful.

MR ARISTOTLE ONASSIS

The late Greek shipping tycoon demonstrated that the combination of good taste and a great tailor (in his case the legendary Caraceni of Milan) can overcome any physical imperfections that God bestows upon a man. Mr Onassis' elegance should bury forever the old myth that big men should avoid double-breasted suits, something that undoubtedly relates to his jacket's low buttoning point and the four-by-two or Kent button stance.

COUNT SIMONE RUCELLAI

In the 30 years since this shot was taken Count Rucellai has had to sell his Tuscan mansion, so let's remember him as a young man proud to be the owner of a BMW motorbike. His perfectly cut tan suit contrasts with the eye-catching helmet – which seems unlikely to make it onto the count's head, given the care that's gone into his hairstyle. We like the way Mr Slim Aarons framed the shot, but we admire the dark shade of the count's brown shoes even more.

MR WILLIAM FAULKNER

The author of *The Sound and the Fury* wasn't just notable for his literary style. His neat snow-white hair, salt-and-pepper Donegal tweeds and extravagant moustache epitomise the look of a mid-century man of letters. Aside from the pipe, the thing that most dates the shot is the evident weight of Mr Faulkner's tweed suit. We also admire the formal double cuffs on his shirt and the pocket square that echoes the colour of his hair.

MR DAVE BRUBECK

The late Mr Dave Brubeck is a jazz icon, and the man behind *Time Out*, the genre's first million-selling album. As a star of the genre with the best-dressed musicians, Mr Brubeck needed to look good, something he initially achieved in soft-shouldered suits and skinny ties. However, and perhaps as a result of his Californian upbringing, he also had an affection for more casual styles, such as this vividly printed shirt.

MR YVES SAINT LAURENT

Now that the late French designer's brand is directed by Mr Hedi Slimane, it's easier to judge Monsieur Yves Saint Laurent's enviable personal style. The enduring influence of Monsieur Saint Laurent, who died in 2008, is such that his rumpled cotton double-breasted suit, with its patch hip pockets and wide lapels, would have wowed the street-style photographers at the Pitti Uomo fashion fair this summer, and any summer.

MR ALEX TURNER

The singer from Arctic Monkeys has come a long way from the 20-year-old who collected the 2006 Mercury Music Prize in a charcoal T-shirt and jeans. His current 1950s-inspired image is part biker, part teddy boy, part Elvis, and is as successful as the Monkeys' superb album *AM*.

MR GEORGE HAMILTON

These days Mr George Hamilton is best known for the depth of his perma-tan, but look beyond the teak-oil façade and you'll see a man with an unswerving devotion to dressing well. He was a customer of London's late celebrity tailor Mr Douglas Hayward, and retains the grip on classic style that he's been demonstrating for 50 years.

MR JAMIE HINCE

The British guitarist, whose biography is curiously obscure given he's married to one of the most beautiful women in the world, has been making records, most notably with The Kills, for the past 20 years. His dedication to rock'n'roll has never been in doubt, and his style reflects this. With his skinny jeans, winkle-picker boots, striped T-shirts and black leather biker jackets he reminds us that rebellion can be chic.

HAPPY BIRTHDAY MUSTANG

MR PORTER celebrates Ford's
working-class hero

Words by Mr Nigel Case, owner of London's Classic Car Club

CARS that make men wax lyrical tend to be exotic specimens beyond the reach of the average Joe. Aston Martins, Jaguar E-Types, Ferraris – such cars receive the highest accolades but in reality have only ever been accessible to a privileged few. The Ford Mustang is something else entirely: a truly affordable mass-market car that has, since its launch in 1964, become a true legend. The Mustang is an out-and-out movie star, the stuff of dreams – and 2014 saw the American classic hit the big Five-O.

Originally intended as a two-seater, Ford decided the Mustang should have room for passengers in the back to widen its appeal. To keep the price low the car was based on the compact Ford Falcon: hardly a promising start. However, a great marketing opportunity lay in the fact that a box-standard straight six could be bought for a tad more than $2,300, while in 1965 you could also buy the car with a thumping 4.7L 306hp V8 engine. To put it into context, that was 20hp more than an Aston Martin DB5 – and all from a car sporting the humble Ford marque.

In the 1960s, not only was there a great choice of engines, brake and suspension packages, and also auto and stick shift, but there were sporty body styles for all tastes: a standard two-door coupé (known as a notchback), a convertible and my particular favourite, the fastback. The Aston Martin V8 bears an uncanny resemblance to the last of these. With great looks and performance, a huge list of options and an affordable price tag, the Mustang was an instant and phenomenal success, with 22,000 cars selling on the first day and more than a million sold in less than two years.

With a production run that spans 50 years, it's the first-generation cars from 1964, 1965 and 1966 that are widely recognised as the most desirable. The inaugural 1964 car (known as the 64½) through to the 1966 model were by far the lightest and most svelte, and arguably the purest form. As is often the case with model progression, 1967 and 1968 saw increasingly aggressive styling and an even larger choice of engines, all the way up to a monstrous 7L V8 Shelby.

Mr Steve McQueen famously drove a 1968 390 GT fastback when he chased down a Dodge Charger in the celluloid epic *Bullitt*. If the car didn't have iconic status before the film's release, its place in motoring legend was assured thereafter. Although the 1969 and 1970 models were only marginally larger, they look much heftier because they have convex, rather than concave, side panels. While there is no denying they still look great, they somehow lost the edge of the earlier cars. The final run of the "classic" first generation, which ended in 1973, saw the car descend into middle age – becoming even more paunchy and less agile in the process.

By this time a dark cloud in the shape of the 1970s oil crisis was gathering over the US, and the sharp rise in fuel prices sounded the death knell for the classic Mustang. However, Ford is a very successful company for the good reason that it has superb foresight.

Launched in 1974, the new Mustang was much smaller, lighter and more economical than the original. It came with comparatively tiny 2.3 and 2.5L engines. The new Mustang signalled a radical departure from the previous model and they sold like hot cakes in those consumption-conscious times. However, while this model was historically important, today it doesn't have anywhere near the same following as the first-generation cars.

For me, the Mustang has never quite managed to regain the magic of the 1960s original. This was recognised by the designers of 2005's fifth-generation car, which was heavily inspired by the first generation. In fact, first-generation Mustangs offer a great ownership proposition because they are really usable with high performance, four good seats and a large boot. The availability of parts is good and the engineering is pretty straightforward, as you would expect from a mass-market car.

Prices are creeping up but you can still pick up a good V8 notchback for around £15,000, with fastbacks and convertibles from around £20,000. If you want the looks but can live without the power a six-cylinder car can be bagged for 20% less. Considering that 1960s Mercedes SLs are similar in terms of their size and performance (but with only two seats), and now change hands for in excess of £100,000, a Mustang represents pretty remarkable value.

However, men of means could blow a whole lot more on something truly spectacular, as there are plenty of rare and wonderful specials to choose from. In 1966 Hertz unbelievably ordered a fleet of high-performance Shelby GT 350H fastbacks. The cars were usually jet black with gold stripes and were marketed as "Rent-A-Racers". Unsurprisingly they often found their way onto the track while out on hire and many were returned missing high-performance parts. If you can find an authentic GT 350H on the market today (beware, there are lots of replicas out there) you won't get much change out of £250,000.

I have run the Classic Car Club in London for people who want to drive great classic cars, but not look after them, since 1995 and we are rarely without at least one Mustang in the fleet. Currently we have three first-generation cars: two convertibles and a notchback. They are perfect because they are easy to drive; they look beautiful and make the radio redundant due to their inimitable V8 soundtrack. They are universally appreciated and welcomed wherever they go, unlike some of their exotic "nose in the air" counterparts. Ford's working-class hero will always have a place in my heart.

1965 – AN EARLY FORD MUSTANG

1966 – SHELBY GT 350H FASTBACK

1974 – FORD MUSTANG

2015 – FORD MUSTANG

MR BRET EASTON ELLIS

The controversial author on why novels are less important in today's society and working with Mr Kanye West

Words by Mr Sanjiv Bhattacharya

MR BRET EASTON ELLIS walks me into his office, a minimalist room in his 11th-floor apartment on Doheny Drive, the street that separates West Hollywood from Beverly Hills. He settles behind his desk, the view of the city rapidly darkening as the sun sets. His book *American Psycho* has been adapted into a musical in London.

"I haven't seen the rehearsals, I have no idea how it's going to turn out," he says. "But isn't that always the way? The book was licensed to Lionsgate so I gave up control long ago. I don't own those characters any more than Peter Benchley did with *Jaws*." He shrugs, "I'm just watching all this, somewhat amused."

He's amused because when it was written, *American Psycho* was so controversial it was almost not even published, let alone adapted into a hit movie and a musical. The original publishers, Simon & Schuster, dropped him when the hate mail began in earnest, regarding the book's sexual violence.

Needless to say, the hiatus was brief. At 25, Mr Ellis was about as successful as an author can be at that age, having written two bestsellers – *Less Than Zero* and *The Rules of Attraction* – both of which would become movies. He was hailed as part of a "brat pack" of young American authors who were the voice of their generation, Mr Jay McInerney and Ms Tama Janowitz among them. He had money, fame and all that came with it. And he hated it. It was classic second album syndrome in which the young artist is disillusioned by "success", particularly the kind portrayed in aspirational lifestyle magazines. So he wrote *American Psycho* in a rage, ensuring that his protagonist Patrick Bateman listed all the designers, brands and celebrities that obsessed him even as he chopped people to pieces. It was Mr Ellis' way of attacking 1980s consumerism with a hatchet.

"I was in a lot of pain back then," he says. "I was about to be a man, I wanted to fit in, but I found the values and hypocrisies of society horrendous. I think that's what men have connected with. There's a theory of male dissatisfaction in the book, and in *Fight Club* too. You're told to look this way, to have this car and these clothes, but it doesn't fulfill you – it doesn't fill that f***ing hole that you feel!"

Mr Ellis says that he writes to alleviate pain. And that as the pain changes as he gets older, he draws from different wells. *American Psycho* was about becoming a man, but *Glamorama* was more "about losing myself to celebrity and confusion in my thirties". *Lunar Park*, his mock memoir, was about "exorcising the ghost of my father". And his recent novel, *Imperial Bedrooms* – a sequel to *Less Than Zero* – was about the bruising experience of turning his short story collection *The Informers* into a movie. It was a three-to-four-year effort that he wrote and co-produced, but which still tanked horribly for the oldest reason in the book. "The money men took over the creative decisions," he says. "I know! But until you go through it yourself, you think, 'I'm in control, I trust these people...'"

I ask him if there's any relief to be had in just reminding himself, "I'm Bret Easton Ellis!" Perhaps ending with "bitch" for extra effect.

"I wish I had that confidence," he smiles. "I have friends who tell me that I should say that to myself every day. I find men who had a good relationship with their father have that kind of confidence. Men who are neurotic didn't. It colours you for a long time."

Mr Ellis didn't. His father, who died in 1992, had been a realtor who drank and would hit him as a small boy. "He never had faith in me as a writer, even after *Less Than Zero* and *Rules of Attraction*," he says. "He only wanted to get back into my life because I was successful, but he thought they were terrible books, dirty books. That does a number on you."

These days, Mr Ellis is more absorbed in movies than in books. It was partly why he returned to LA in 2006, after 18 years in New York. "The idea of the novel has become much less important in society. But also, the party was over in New York. It was getting too expensive, people were drifting away. And a couple of bad things happened to me, personal stuff." He lost his boyfriend, the sculptor Mr Michael Wade Kaplan, to a heart attack. It was time to come home.

So his days are spent largely with scripts now. Not big studio pictures – "I'm hardly the guy they're going to call to do *Spider-Man*!" – but a handful of indie projects and TV work. It's by no means a smooth ride. His script for *The Canyons*, starring Ms Lindsay Lohan, flopped horribly. But still, he's busy working on a mini-series set in LA in 1969, about some characters with vague connections to the Manson family.

Then there's also a project for Mr Kanye West. "It's the most bizarre thing I've ever written, and I initially said no two, three or four times. But we met a couple of times, and he completely persuaded me."

It makes sense that Kanye would call Bret – both extraordinarily successful in their fields, and yet with an outsider's edge. While many authors graduate into professorships at creative writing programmes, or judging panels for prizes, Mr Ellis does no such thing. "I'm not turning that stuff down," he laughs. "No one offers me that stuff. There's this idea that I'm just too out there. I've never won a literary prize. I'm still the *enfant terrible*. And that's fine until you're about 37 or so. After that, it just becomes embarrassing."

Mr Ellis is 50. Not the cheeriest of ages you'd have thought, but this, of all things, makes him happy.

"Look, your forties are terrible, but I hear that your fifties are really good." He grins. "And then your sixties start sucking, and it's all downhill from there!"

EIGHT TOMES EVERY MAN
SHOULD READ

*Bespoke library expert Mr Philip Blackwell picks
his ultimate reading list*

Words by Mr Tom M Ford

WITH ENDLESS recommendations and enticing bestseller lists, choosing what we want to read can become a dizzying task. Mr Philip Blackwell, founder of Ultimate Library, understands this all too well. A man who has since 2007 supplied the world's hotels, resorts and private residences – from The Savoy in London to Amandari resort in Bali – with bespoke book libraries, he is well versed in creating essential reading lists. With this in mind, we tasked him to come up with the eight books every man should read. Although it's hard for a list of eight tomes to be comprehensive, Mr Blackwell's covers everything from Dickens and Shakespeare to Sir Richard Burton and Mr William Boyd. "Here are my top eight titles for every man's library, to read at leisure or in those interludes before nodding off," he says.

A LITTLE HISTORY OF THE WORLD
EH Gombrich

"A richly satisfying romp through world history that no enquiring mind should be without, nor neglect to re-read from time to time. This books leads the reader through a story of man from the Stone Age to the atomic bomb, focusing on the larger experiences of life across all domains including wars, battles, art and science."

ONE ON ONE – 101 TRUE ENCOUNTERS
Craig Brown

"One hundred and one chance meetings, juxtaposing the famous and the infamous, the artistic and philistine, the pompous and the comical, the snobbish and the vulgar, told by Britain's funniest writer."

THE SONNETS AND NARRATIVE POEMS
William Shakespeare

"The Everyman edition of his sonnets is a distilled greatest hits of our nation's favourite author in one accessible volume, and the perfect way to read Shakespeare."

I AM PILGRIM
Terry Hayes

"Escaping within the pages of a good thriller is a necessity from time to time. A most absorbing read, *I Am Pilgrim* explores the challenges faced by the former head of a secret espionage unit for US intelligence. From a public beheading in Mecca to the unexplored wilderness of the Hindu Kush, *Pilgrim* takes the reader on an unparalleled yet realistic adventure."

CHURCHILL
Roy Jenkins

"The definitive warts-and-all portrait of the greatest ever Briton. It serves to remind us that it is best to judge a man by his actions and achievements, not by his perhaps-flawed personality."

THE DEVIL DRIVES –
A LIFE OF SIR RICHARD BURTON
Fawn M Brodie

"The dazzling riches of Sir Richard Burton's life takes us back to an earlier, golden age of travel and exploration. Master of 29 languages, a prolific writer, pioneer, sexual psychologist and spy, we feel humbled by his achievements."

GREAT EXPECTATIONS
Charles Dickens

"Dickens' masterpiece runs the gamut of human emotions: hope, despair, love, hate, jealousy, generosity. It is a richly populated, fast-paced story of rags to riches and is as relevant today as it was when written more than a century ago."

ANY HUMAN HEART
William Boyd

"A brilliantly crafted novel that combines both a moving personal account and a history of the art and politics of the 20th century. The masterpiece of one of the greatest living novelists."

MESSRS ANTHONY AND
NICHOLAS HOROWITZ

*One is a world-renowned writer, the other a sporty history
graduate – father and son talk about collaborating on
the* Alex Rider *books and their contrasting views on style*

Words by Mr Rob Ryan

AT 59, Mr Anthony Horowitz, who was awarded an OBE for
services to literature in 2014, is one of the UK's most prolific
and successful authors and screenwriters. He is the creator
of the Alex Rider teen spy series and of the long-running TV
series *Foyle's War*. He also wrote *The House of Silk*, the first new

Sherlock Holmes novel approved by the Conan Doyle Estate. His elder son, Mr Nicholas Horowitz, is 25, graduated with a first in history from Edinburgh University and is studying the financial side of film-making. Here, father and son talk about how the younger Mr Horowitz's sporting prowess has influenced his dad's work, and the joy of a new shirt.

Nick, what effect has Anthony's career had on you?
NICK: Because he was writing books aimed at my age group, there was a constant request for autographs from classmates. In fact, that's pretty much continued throughout my life, as he gradually became known for teen and adult books and TV series, as well as his children's series.

Anthony, have your sons affected your work?
ANTHONY: I always tried to involve both the boys [Nicholas has a brother, Mr Cassian Horowitz, who's two years younger] in my world, simply because my father didn't. I wasn't sure what he did exactly, he was rather a distant figure. They have both ended up in the world of media, and that can't be a coincidence, but I never pushed them in that direction.

Anthony, is it true that Nick has had a significant input into your work?
ANTHONY: It is. I've always thought of this as a family business. Both of my sons read every book and make suggestions. Cass is very forthright. I remember having to rewrite 30,000 words after he'd finished with one draft of a novel. Nick is more generous in his appraisals. But what Nick brought to Alex Rider was the sheer physicality of the character. Whenever Alex goes skiing or snowboarding or windsurfing, that's all from watching Nicholas. There's a lot of Nick in Alex.
NICK: Ever since I can remember, I've had an excess of energy. I love sports, from rugby and football to swimming and skiing. I have to stay active.

ANTHONY: Whereas I don't do anything like that. My idea of relaxing after a day's writing is to write some more. I'm much more cerebral than Nick. I sometimes wonder where that extraordinary sporting gene came from. But the other thing Nick brought to the work is that he enabled me to understand how teenagers think, which was very important. Not speak – nothing dates like current slang – but knowing how someone his age sees the world was vital to making Alex believable.

If you don't share a love of sport, what do you share a passion for? Music?
ANTHONY: I'm the only one in the family who likes classical music.
NICK: Because my generation has access to so many different genres, we don't limit ourselves to just one – so I'll listen to classical, pop, hip-hop, rock and rap. We don't see musical boundaries the way older generations do.
ANTHONY: That's a good point, I'd never thought of that. Film is something we both love.
NICK: I enjoy the way I can come to Dad and mention a style of film or a plot and he'll pull out an old Buster Keaton movie or an obscure Hitchcock, something I know nothing about.
ANTHONY: What we do share is an absolute compulsion to do whatever we do to the best of our ability. In my case that only applies to writing – with Nick it's a whole range of activities.

What about clothes? Do you each have a particular style?
ANTHONY: I'm very much a jeans and T-shirt man. I have been known to wear a suit, but it's not my attire of choice.
NICK: Whereas I like putting on a suit. In the last place I worked, a sports and entertainment agency, I was seen as a bit odd in that way – people would say: "When is the interview?" because the ethos was much more casual. But I find nice clothes give me confidence. I like an open collar under a suit, or a bow tie. And I like wearing a dinner jacket – it's that feeling of dressing up in something really quite formal that makes you feel good.

Do either of you have a clothing indulgence?

NICK: With me, it's a white shirt. My mother always laughs because I have so many. I love a fresh, crisp white shirt, although you can guarantee I'll spill something down a new one within seconds of putting it on. Just once, oddly, like I have to christen it.

ANTHONY: I have rather a lot of T-shirts. But I do like expensive clothes. I love the finish and the fabrics. As I get older I find I'm narrowing down my choices. I'd rather have two or three really nice items than a whole wardrobe full of designer clothes. And I don't like anything with a prominent logo. What I always say is that well-made clothes are a good investment because they last so much longer.

NICK: That's true and I find that if you've paid a lot for something you look after it, maybe put it straight onto a hanger when you take it off. If it's cheap, you tend to drop it on the floor at the end of the day.

Have you always had a warm and easy relationship, or were there rocky adolescent years?

ANTHONY: We are two very different individuals who have always been incredibly close. I can honestly say we have never really fallen out. Disagreements, perhaps; differences of opinion, certainly, but nothing more serious than that.

NICK: Going away to boarding school when I was 13 helped. Not being in each other's hair all the time gave us all some space to appreciate each other when we got back together.

ANTHONY: It was strange because we talked a lot about whether Nick should board, and I was all for it while my wife Jill [Green, film producer] was much less convinced. And then when he went, it was me who ended up missing Nick the most. But it meant when we were together, we only had fun. And we still do.

BACK-TO-WORK PLAYLIST

Award-winning music consultant Mr Rob Wood selects the
perfect soundtrack to get you into the swing of things

WE OFTEN KNOW what a brand or space looks like, but how
should it sound? As creative director and founder of award-
winning consultancy Music Concierge, Mr Rob Wood certainly
knows. Music Concierge offers bespoke music programming for
boutique hotels, luxury brands, members' clubs and more. Using
a library that spans "120 genres, from 17th-century baroque
through rare jazz to cutting-edge electronica", Mr Wood has
selected a playlist to enliven your commute and inspire your
working day.

"Don't Give Up"
WASHED OUT

"Dolly Parton's '9 to 5' might have been a more obvious choice, but this slow-burning, romantic and feel-good piece of electronica will get you through the day."

"We No Who U R"
NICK CAVE & THE BAD SEEDS

"Are you finding it hard to concentrate? Empty your head of all pop junk and instead immerse yourself in Cave's ethereal record. It's good for the soul."

"Falling"
HAIM

"Easily one of the most exciting pop-rock bands to hit my ears recently, this song makes every day feel like a Saturday."

"A Lot of Love"
STEVE MASON

"The ex-Beta Band front man has made a wonderful, angry and political album [*Monkey Minds in the Devil's Times*] that will shake the cobwebs out of the most pickled mind."

"Golden Clouds"
THE ORB FEATURING LEE "SCRATCH" PERRY

"A brilliant meeting of out-there minds that is as zany and creative as it is inspiring."

"I Was An Eagle"
LAURA MARLING

"The fourth album [*Once I Was An Eagle*] from this young, super talented folk singer is her most accomplished yet. Tracks such as this are a lovely intimate companion to early blurry-eyed mornings."

"Let's Work"
PRINCE

"If anyone knows how to motivate the troops, it's the purple one."

"Waiting for the Train"
FLASH AND THE PAN

"Fab early 1980s new-wave pop from down under. This is dedicated to everyone forced to experience the joys of public transport on a daily basis."

"Portrait"
JOSEPHINE

"This young Mancunian has sassy maturity way beyond her years on this pitch-perfect pop single. On even the most blue of Mondays, this is guaranteed to cheer you up."

"Journey in Satchidananda"
ALICE COLTRANE

"With an intricate and dazzlingly beautiful piece of harp playing by John Coltrane's wife, Alice, this Indo-jazz track is the perfect way to clear your mind as you walk home from a hard day's work."

MR YVES BÉHAR

The pioneering designer behind Jawbone's UP24 wristband reveals tomorrow's tech innovations

Words by Mr Aaron Britt

AS FOUNDER AND CEO of the New York- and San Francisco-based design and strategy firm fuseproject, Mr Yves Béhar has staked his place atop the design world at the incredibly fruitful intersection of technological innovation and human experience.

The Swiss-born designer's bold-faced clients include Mini, Prada, Puma, PayPal, Herman Miller, Google and scores of others, but it's the human interactions with those products that you're most likely to remember – running your finger along the sinuous curves of his Leaf lamp for Herman Miller to activate the LEDs, marvelling at the wireless sound emanating from a Jambox speaker, tracking your activity with a UP24 wearable for Jawbone, reclining into the suspension bridge-inspired back of a SAYL office chair and the effervescent spurt of a SodaStream.

A restless innovator, Mr Béhar's impact on the design and tech sectors resounds. He's won a prestigious National Design Award, was dubbed one of *Time* magazine's 25 Style & Design Visionaries, and his work has found a home in the collections of some of the world's leading art and design museums.

MR PORTER visited Mr Béhar's studio to ask him about where he sees design's chance to better the world, and what taking the time to go surfing means to him.

You've been adept at marrying object and technology. How do you think about that intersection?

Design and technology have the greatest potential to change the human experience when combined. Different disciplines of design need to be combined, or "fused" as we say at fuseproject, in order to achieve breakthroughs: user experience, industrial design and brand address the design opportunity at once, looking to solve the idiosyncrasies of modern life. Products and experiences need to have a big idea behind them, one that will set them apart from a cluttered environment. Good designers work like editors: reducing the features, creating a simple yet compelling experience, addressing users with emotional intelligence, making sure that every design element that is left is to the service of the big idea.

You've worked extensively with Herman Miller and Jawbone. What's the key to a long-term and fruitful collaboration with a client?

The best work is done with people you know, and companies you have fully internalised as a designer. And since design work is never done, companies will always need to evolve; it's a huge asset to have a long-term relationship with a designer.

My passion is to do the best work possible, so very early on I knew that long-term relationships were going to allow me to simply push my work to new places. By being dedicated to one client, I can think both about what the company needs in five to 10 years, and position current and immediate work so we can deliver on the future vision. The work you see emerging now with Herman Miller and Jawbone are visions from five or 10 years ago that together we shared and pursued.

You've done some great furniture design, but can you talk us through what sets the MultipliCITY line for Landscape Forms apart?

MultipliCITY for Landscape Forms is our first outdoor furniture collection, and it wants to be beautiful and place-creating, while at the same time offering other designers flexibility to achieve their own visions. It was designed as a creative canvas. That is why we focused on an environmentally efficient set of legs and supports for the benches, tables and bike racks, and then we let local architects make the call on what best indigenous material to use for the horizontal surfaces (seats and table tops).

Where does MultipliCITY live within the furniture you've designed?
It fits with our other furniture work as it is graphically simple and strong from afar, yet subtle form transitions make it something people will appreciate when in close contact. We also wanted to acknowledge that today the outdoors is used for both leisure and for work. So the ergonomics of the seats and the functional details of the bike racks take into account that we have technology with us. The bike racks have a counter-height surface that provides a shelf while locking one's bike. Much better than setting your bags and helmet on the asphalt!

How does life in the Bay Area inform your work?
Northern California is an incredible source of calm in my life, which I have to balance with the constant excitement of new creative frontiers. Surfing is a very Zen practice for me, seeing the shore from the water presents a different perspective, something I am used to doing in my work: to look at things from a new angle. San Francisco and the Bay Area are unique in this way, at the same time grounded in beautiful and abundant nature, and propelled into the future by new ideas.

You're strongly interested in social innovation. Can you tell me about design's opportunity to make real change?
There are so many opportunities for design to make a difference, both in the for-profit world and in the non-profit space. Everything needs to be redesigned, and when one experiences the world, it is pretty clear that much can be improved for the majority of our societies. I honestly don't see a difference between both

practices. All I know is that design can look at problems from a human standpoint, and that creates value that is both tangible and intangible.

Can you talk us through a couple of these social innovation design projects?
I am particularly involved with education and health projects all around the world. There are now millions of XO laptops and tablets from One Laptop Per Child being used in education systems in 40 countries, and millions of eyeglasses designed for Augen in Mexico and the US that allow kids to see and learn. In health, we are working on future technologies to diagnose and treat endemic diseases such as malaria and on young women's issues in Africa as well. It's all hard work, but it's increasingly important for designers to apply their game-changing craft in the places where we can make the most difference.

How do you think about design and the human body? How do you design for intimate contact?
The hardest things to design are wearables, both technically and from a personal style standpoint. It is not enough to be on-trend; in fact, for most wearables we need to create our own trend. I think this is what makes fashion scared of tech, and tech scared of fashion: it's a new language that does not reside in either camp. It needs to be invented.

TECH TRIBES

The tech world is in need of a sartorial reboot.
It's time to download Geek Chic 3.0

Words by Mr Ben Machell

IT ALL KICKED OFF around 2010. Prior to that, if I was ever asked
to interview a successful, famous and wealthy young man, then
they would invariably be one of three things: a singer, an actor or
a sportsman. But then my editors cottoned on to the emergence
of a new group, of wan-faced boys who didn't just know about the
internet, but who knew how to make huge amounts of money off
the back of it too. And, just like that, I was off, sent to New York,
to San Francisco, to east London in order to interview these guys
and possibly even encourage them to make eye contact now and
then. And the irony was that while even bottom-rung actors,
singers and sportsmen would employ entire platoons of stylists,
these thrusting twentysomething geeks could buy and sell nations
but still looked pretty much like, well, twentysomething geeks.
Still, the deeper into their world I got, the more distinction I was
able to observe between the different types of players and the
more familiar I was able to get with the various stylistic tropes on
display. So if you're involved in this world – or if you plan to be –
then hopefully what follows will provide some basic pointers as to
where the competition is going wrong. At least in terms of clothes.

THE CEOS

We can break these guys down into three groups. The first made their millions and, realising they were being photographed in cargo shorts a little too often, suddenly decided to make some stylish investments: cue Twitter's Mr Jack Dorsey stepping out in Dior and Tumblr's Mr David Karp upgrading to crisp shirts and blazers. Job done. At the other end of the spectrum are the tech ascetics, the dotcom gurus who, as a point of pride, wear the same thing every day, whether it's Mr Mark Zuckerberg's limitless supply of grey T-shirts, Mr Steve Jobs' turtleneck and New Balance sneakers or Mr Bill Gates' Oxford shirt and V-neck team. They have no time for concerns such as "What should I wear today?" when they are working towards a higher purpose. And lastly, we have those who insist on wearing clothing with their company logo printed all over. It's sweet, but a bit like seeing a band wearing their own tour T-shirts. Golden rule: you never wear the merch!

UPDATES AVAILABLE

While we're firm believers that once a man runs the company he can enjoy dressing as he damn well pleases, we also think that he should give some thought as to what might please other people. Dare we say it? There's more to life than a baggy black turtleneck, starting with an unstructured blazer and some penny loafers.

THE START-UP GRUNTS

The whole hoodie and flip-flop thing may now exist as a catch-all sartorial cliché for young tech bucks, but trust me, it's a cliché for good reason. From Palo Alto to Shoreditch's Silicon Roundabout this aesthetic is unavoidable among the bleary-eyed coders who graft away in some start-up incubator-cum-sweatshop. One part homage to early Zuckerberg (they call him "Zuck" and, deep down, adore him), one part practical consideration (when you live in your office, you want to be comfortable), pizza and coffee stains serve as ostentatious badges of honour, like medals on a North Korean general. There is though, a large amount of sartorial groupthink at play: fleeces and Crocs just about pass muster for these guys, ditto T-shirts with HTML references that you are absolutely not meant to understand. Apparently, snazzy socks are the one area where self-expression is permitted, which is either encouraging or depressing, depending on how you think about it.

UPDATES AVAILABLE

We're ambitious here at MR PORTER, but not so ambitious that we think we can persuade young programmers to abandon the comfortable styles to which they're so wedded. We merely suggest that the fits and fabrics of their hoodies and tees are upgraded.

THE VENTURE CAPITALISTS

I'd always assumed these guys just wore pinstripe suits and walked around with briefcases of cash handcuffed to their wrists, but then I met a load in California the other year and all they talked about was skydiving and going to Burning Man. They'd made their money in The Valley and had recast themselves as nicely tanned New-Age outdoorsmen, acting (and dressing) as if they had a direct Bluetooth connection to the ghost of Mr Jim Morrison reciting the FTSE index. So expect lots of beads, lots of those shoes that aren't quite hiking boots but aren't quite trainers either, lots of wearable hemp, lots of bobble beanie hats and plenty of Native American accessorising. It's not that they're embarrassed by their past lives as sun-starved code-monkeys; it's just that they've been on a spiritual journey that involved a wildly successful IPO and a trip to a Tesla electric sports car showroom.

UPDATES AVAILABLE

What could be nicer than having the money to dress in expensive clothes that are as comfy as sweatpants? These neo-hippies can lead the lives we all dream of, and dress accordingly in handmade cashmere, rugged sneakers and ethnic-inspired jewellery.

THE "WEARABLE TECH" TYPES

I mean, on one level, yes, very good, we get it: technology is your life, and what says "technology is my life!" more than incorporating as much of it as is physically possible into your wardrobe? So, Google Glass? Check. Smartwatch? Check. Bluetooth ring that lets you respond to text messages with simple, though possibly quite campy, gestures? Check. A turtleneck sweater fitted with an LED light that changes colour depending on your mood? Ch... wait... hang on, a turtleneck sweater that changes colour depending on your mood? Yes, they exist. Yes, people wear them. Just... just think about that. See where this leads? It might begin with an innocent love of gadgets and charming lack of self-awareness but before long you're not so much an "early adopter" as someone cosplaying a dystopian future in which nobody has sex and everyone's terrified of rain. Wearable tech is, at best, "fun", not "fashion".

UPDATES AVAILABLE

Just because you can doesn't mean you should. In other words we're opposed to turtlenecks with mood-controlled LEDs, and opposed to tech specs unless they look as good as regular ones. But before we're dismissed as Luddites please note we were early adopters of wearable tech, in the form of fine watches, great headphones, beautiful pens and, more recently, Google Glass.

THE PROFESSIONAL TED SPEAKER

They could be anyone from a beatific design guru rhapsodising about "the science of beauty" to a tousle-haired college dropout who struck it lucky with his first app. But beyond their crisp hand gestures, uncanny ease with wearable microphones and knack for bumper sticker motivation ("Fail well"), these tech televangelists will often share style references. So expect a nod to on-stage formality with an off-the-rail shirt and jacket, only undercut with jeans or a pair of Converse, or pretty much anything that says, "I've learnt to do things on my terms, even if that means looking a bit like I'm showing up for my first day of work experience". And the cherry on the top? Unquestionably expensive glasses, just so there is absolutely no doubt that you are both rich and smart. Because if you're not both of those things, who in this world is going to listen to a single word you say?

UPDATES AVAILABLE

Tech gurus might pride themselves on their bold new business models, but even the most innovative people benefit from being well presented. If you are going to take to the stage and make people look at you please do so in a well-fitting blazer and jeans.

MR DAMON ALBARN

The restless musician talks exclusively, and candidly,
about his haunting debut solo album

Words by Mr Dan Cairns

THE CLATTER AND CLANG of a passing train drown out the birdsong that has, until now, filled the air. In the distance, the Westway is, as ever, choked with traffic. Surveying this, on the penthouse terrace that stretches the width of his west London HQ, Mr Damon Albarn and I spark up cigarettes and revel in the sun.

Three floors below the terrace lies the recording studio where, in 2013, Mr Albarn made *Everyday Robots* – his very first solo album, and a record described as one of the greatest pieces of music this restless, inquisitive, multifaceted musician has produced. Don't unroll the bunting or hit the dance floor just yet, though. *Everyday Robots* is also the most personal and, for the most part, downbeat record Mr Albarn has made to date. To understand what inspired its spare, forlorn and deeply reflective lyrics, melodies and soundscapes, we need to follow its writer far, far back to his childhood in Leytonstone, east London, to the streets, parks and woodland he explored, to the multicultural community he grew up in. Mr Albarn did just that while writing the album, walking around his old haunts.

"It was very low-key," the singer says. "I just got on the tube, got out at Leytonstone, walked around, smoked. It helped me realise that the majority of my memories of that time are pretty joyous, really. What I learnt from making the record was that I now understand what happened to me; this happy, boyish, very open kid, living in a very fresh-feeling, multicultural neighbourhood, with a good, strong set of influences, in my house, next door, down the road." That all came to an end when Mr Albarn was nine, and he went on holiday to Turkey with a friend of his parents while they and his sister moved to an Essex village, leading to the start of a radically different life for Mr Albarn on his return. "I had this mad sort of mini-odyssey in Turkey," the 46-year-old continues, "and then came back to Anglo-Saxon rural Essex. And I went to the village school, tanned, from multicultural London, and immediately I was an outsider. And that sense didn't diminish, it grew. I think now that that was the point where I started to become consciously creative. And I do think there needs to be some sort of disturbance in your psyche for creativity to be sparked. I understand that now – and everything preceding that, and since it, begins to make sense. That's why making the record has been so great. It's like, finally, I get it."

Yet there are other things that Mr Albarn doesn't get at all, as the lyrics on *Everyday Robots* make clear. The title track is self-evidently bleak, with lines – set to mournful descending piano chords, over which a classical-violin sample hovers menacingly – such as "We're everyday robots in control, or in the process of being sold" attesting to the singer's preoccupation with, and fear about, what mankind's retreat behind mobile phones, tablets and computers, and into a sort of catatonic state of alienation, denial and disconnection, will mean for our collective future.

Mr Richard Russell – owner of XL Records – was charged with editing down the 60 songs or song sketches that Mr Albarn gave him. He was also a crucial contributor as *Everyday Robots'* producer, his armoury of strange samples and beats pushing Mr Albarn way beyond his comfort zone.

Another key intervention by Mr Russell concerned the album's major curveball, "Mr Tembo" – a song about an orphaned elephant

Mr Albarn met while visiting Tanzania with Mr Paul Simonon, the former bass player of The Clash. Within the context of *Everyday Robots*, it serves as a necessary tension breaker, undoubtedly. But it is also utterly delightful, as the singer, backed by Leytonstone City Mission Choir (whom he first heard when cycling past their church as a child), shakes off the surrounding introspection and simply throws himself at the song. "That's totally there as a result of Richard," Mr Albarn says. "I saw it as being very much in the 'music for kids' category – I've written a lot of songs for my daughter over the years. So I was like, 'Come on, I'm not going to record that'. But Richard went, 'You have to'. They seem particularly keen on that one in the States, and want to make a really special video for it." When Mr Albarn sang the song to the elephant, it emptied its bowels. Will that detail be included in the video? "I don't think you can get an elephant to crap on demand," Mr Albarn laughs. "But seriously, I can't begin to describe how strong the aroma was. We were in a camp in the middle of the wilderness, the elephant's there with his handler, and I'm stood there with Paul, who doesn't have a sense of smell, so he was fine. On the original version, you can almost hear me retching as I'm singing. The only time I've encountered a stench as bad as that was when a tomcat sat on my chest, turned round and sprayed in my face. I mean, I saw stars. I entered the universe of catdom at that moment."

Let's go back to Turkey, though, and a nine-year-old boy "wandering around on my own", as the singer puts it, "walking into mosques and drinking tea in carpet shops". That visit sounds like a hugely significant experience in terms of how it inculcated in him a desire, and a willingness, to investigate and draw upon influences, and use them in his work. A natural magpie, Mr Albarn exhibits all the signs of wanting to recreate the multicultural life he grew up with in east London, before that "disturbance", as he describes it. Well, long may he recreate, long may he dig, and long may he roam.

NOTE TO SELF

Taking "selfies" has become a global phenomenon,
but is it always a good idea for a grown man?

Words by Mr Dan Davies

I WAS A RELATIVE LATECOMER to Instagram but have embraced it with enthusiasm; this despite getting routinely teased about my output being, in effect, a photographic blog of my daughter.

In my defence, I argue that my following on Instagram is a tiny fraction of what it is on Twitter (which, in itself, is nothing for Kim Kardashian to worry about) and posting photos is an easy way to ensure friends and far-flung relatives can keep abreast of her development. Plus, she's undeniably cute and as a doting father I'm not ashamed to share this fact. So much so that I have been known to take the occasional "selfie" of us together.

"Selfie" was named word of the year for 2013 by Oxford Dictionaries. The practice of standing in a public place or in front of a mirror, arm outstretched awkwardly (or in my case, wrestling a want-away toddler like a small alligator), has become so ubiquitous that usage of the word increased by 17,000% in the year leading up to October 2013. But what does this fad say about humanity, what does it say about men, and, in this age of rampant narcissism, what does it say about me? Some experts argue that the selfie is emblematic of the need to record, edit and share having overcome our willingness to experience and reflect. Others insist it indicates an overarching desire to control how we want the world to see us. Then there are those who believe the selfie is a natural extension to the all-encompassing cult of celebrity, being photographed as a validation of status. In his article in *The New York Times*, the actor and "selfie king" Mr James Franco (*@JamesFrancoTV*) put it more succinctly: "Attention is power".

Illness might be a more appropriate term. Neuroscientists have known for some time that our obsession with checking emails derives from primitive human instincts – and Instagram thrives on much the same addictive behaviour. We're searchers by nature and each time we find a bit of information – an incoming message or the orange notification that someone has liked one of our pictures – we are rewarded with a tiny squirt of dopamine, the pleasure-producing chemical in our brains.

What this means is our world of constant connection – and yes, that includes the compulsion to see how many people have liked the picture of you showing off your new car or gym-ripped physique – is turning you into a lab rat. I know because I feel the dopamine pulsing through my body every time someone likes a picture of my daughter.

Evidence of humanity's descent into attention-deficit chaos might be expected from the Instagram accounts of Hollywood stars, or indeed pop idols, reality TV wannabes and underwear models (some of which are really rather good), but the surge in popularity of selfies among "ordinary men" is a more interesting social phenomenon.

A survey found that British males are twice as likely to take selfies as women, suggesting that along with make-up, the pressures of body image and the fastidious maintenance of eyebrows, we can now celebrate the absorption into our culture of the impulse to pout in front of the camera. What's more, research reveals that before posting pictures of themselves men are more likely to edit them to make them look better. So we can add vanity to the list, too.

It is my experience of being a man that we are not predisposed to enjoying the good fortune of our fellow men, especially when it is advertised to us through our devices. Scroll through your Instagram feed and alight on a perfectly framed shot of a friend's suntanned feet protruding from the bottom of a sun-lounger, the aquamarine of the Indian Ocean twinkling in the background. Stop and peruse selfies that take in the view from an executive box at the biggest sporting event in town, from the top of a mountain after a particularly arduous bike ride or with an arm casually slung around the waist of a famous woman. I defy you not to think: "Bastard" or "Show-off". Such images – now known as "braggies" – make us jealous, resentful and feel bad about ourselves.

Men, of course, are naturally competitive but self-admiration and braggadocio are to be guarded against. It is therefore time to stop the slide and reclaim the high ground from the mirror-seekers and the goldfish-minded. We should return to taking and sharing funny photos, pictures of stunning landscapes, buildings or our shoes, and, when they let us, of our children (without, from this point on, fathers like me pulling them into the frame).

But what if you're still feeling the urge to lift one arm, look into the lens and hope it doesn't catch your bald patch? I urge you to follow the example of one man who has captured the essence of the male selfie: Mr Benny Winfield Jr, AKA *@mrpimpgoodgame*. His modus operandi and 125,000-plus followers should be a lesson to us all.

SHORE THING

Crashing waves, beautiful sunsets and ever-changing views are guaranteed with a beach house. Here's our selection…

Words by Mr Nick Compton

WHO DOESN'T DREAM of their own beach retreat, opening onto sea and sand with nothing to get in the way? Who doesn't summon up Bali, Malibu or the Mumbles, surfboards, Labradors and beach towels at times of high stress or high wind-chill factor? We all want a beach house. And there is pretty much a beach house to suit everyone.

From steamy huts to sturdy windswept cottages, corrugated shacks to grandiloquent piles, the beach house is peculiarly specific to its place; they tend to follow the local vernacular and respond to the local climate and conditions. They sit on stilts or seek shelter from the storm. Beach-house styles are many and various but for the past 50 or so years, one particular style has held sway: the modernist glass box. As the American *Arts & Architecture* magazine noted way back in 1955: "Most vacation houses are designed to work, roughly, like a camera: a box, glazed on one side, with the glass wall pointed at the view."

It is a style you see explored and extrapolated on from Camps Bay to Camber Sands, Punta del Este to Perth but most notably in California and the northeast coast of the US. Messrs Andrew Geller and Charles Gwathmey redefined the beach house in the 1950s and 1960s, creating a string of modest modernist gems on

Martha's Vineyard and Long Island and the beach-house form has been played with by architects ever since, from Mr Richard Meier to Messrs Álvaro Siza, Tadao Ando and Marcio Kogan. Some things stay constant though: the urge to bring in as much of the sea as possible; the colour, the smell, the breeze and the bouncing light.

LA MAISON AU BORD DE L'EAU
Miami (temporarily), US

The late Ms Charlotte Perriand is one of the most celebrated and collectable of the European mid-century designers, her work now sells for a very *grand prix*. In 1934 she entered her design for La Maison au Bord de l'Eau in a magazine competition to find designs for cheap-to-build holiday homes. Ms Perriand came second and the house was never built. Until now. Working from original sketches and drawings, Louis Vuitton installed Ms Perriand's design at the Raleigh Hotel during December 2013's Design Miami show. There's no news to date on whether the house will have a more permanent location.

PARATY HOUSE
Paraty, Brazil

The Brazilian architect Mr Marcio Kogan has created some of
the world's most desirable residences. And none more so than
this elegant pair of concrete boxes, set on the thickly jungled
mountainside of one of the islands of Paraty, between Rio and São
Paulo. The lower of the two boxes is open to the elements, mostly
benign in these parts, and to the beach. The rooms in the upper
box are shielded from the sun by eucalyptus-stick *brise-soleil*. And
if the views, the sea, the beach and the pool weren't enough, the
house also boasts a fine collection of 20th-century furniture and
contemporary art.

CASA KIKÉ
Cahuita, Costa Rica

Designed by UK-based architect Mr Gianni Botsford, Casa Kiké is set in the Costa Rican jungle, a short stumble to the Caribbean coast. It was built for his father, a writer, former academic and friend of Mr Saul Bellow. The house is essentially two massive bookcases: angled boxes built in timber and clad in corrugated steel, lifted four feet off the ground and connected by a 50ft elevated walkway. Remarkably, the budget for the entire project was £55,000.

MANLY STREET BEACH HOUSE
Paraparaumu, New Zealand

Given its 9,400 miles of coastline, New Zealand has almost as many beach houses as sheep. Most of them are relatively modest and tagged "baches" after bachelor pad. The Manly Street Beach House is a super-bach, designed by architect Mr Gerald Parsonson for his own family. Set among sand dunes, with views of Kapiti Island, and a short stroll from the sea, the house uses traditional "bach" materials. But Mr Parsonson has used them to create a lovely low-slung modernist jumble, suggesting a camp site, he says, topped off with a crow's-nest tower for watching whales by day and stars by night.

THE SHINGLE HOUSE
Dungeness, UK

The strange moonscape shingle of Dungeness in Kent can feel like a long way from Malibu, especially if Dungeness B nuclear power station is in your sightline. But it is developing a cluster of architecturally interesting buildings, such as The Shingle House designed by Scottish practice NORD. The building, a series of oversized beach huts, was commissioned by Living Architecture, Mr Alain de Botton's project to create beguiling spaces for hire in beguiling places. The interior is comprised of chic oak and concrete, and sleeps eight, if you're interested in staying in the UK's only official desert.

LEFEVRE HOUSE
Punta Misterio, Peru

The Lefevre House in Punta Misterio, 75 miles south of Lima, juts out of the desert and over the Pacific coast. Designed by Longhi Architects, the house is all angles and stark minimalism with the main living area in a hanging glass box. And while it is far from modest in scale of execution, rooftop sand gardens blend it backwards into the desert while swimming pools dissolve into the seaview. The house's position means that every room has an ocean view, while a side entrance leads to stairs cut into the cliff that descend to the beach.

SMITH HOUSE
Connecticut, US

The American architect Mr Richard Meier has been designing
some of America's finest beach houses, among grander projects,
for almost half a century. One of his first houses, designed when
he was only 31 and completed two years later in 1967, is the Smith
House, a white modernist cube built on the Connecticut stretch
of Long Island Sound. Clearly influenced by Le Corbusier, the
house is mostly glass and air with a triple-height living space that
has views onto the Sound. A circular staircase leads to the garden
from which steps descend to the private beach.

MODERN LOVE

*Five men – from single to long-time married – reveal exactly
what the "L word" means to them*

Words by Mr Chris Elvidge

LOVE. It makes the world go round. It's all you need. But what
exactly does it mean to the modern man?

We spoke to five men – three singletons, one in a long-term
relationship, and one who has been married for more than 40 years
– to find out just that.

MR DAVID MCKENDRICK

Mr McKendrick is the creative director of British *Esquire*. He is 37 years old and single at the time of writing, although he has recently discovered the delights of Tinder, and spends much of our interview fielding texts from last night's date. Suffice to say, it seems to have gone rather well.

What does love mean to you?
Love's a lot of different things. I certainly think that in my experience there seem to be a couple of different types of love. There's one that can be selfish and quite crippling, and then there's the one that becomes the outpouring of the good inside you. The second is the preferable one, of course.

Are you a romantic guy?
I think so. But perhaps you should ask some of the girls I've dated! They might beg to differ.

What do you think it means?
I think small things can be romantic. Someone bringing you breakfast in bed, or a cup of tea. Little things that when added up amount to something bigger. I don't believe in subscribing to this idea of heavy gestures... I try not to be ostentatious.

What has been the defining relationship of your life so far?
I was in a 10-year relationship between the ages of 23 and 33. And she is now probably one of my best friends.

What did you learn from that?
I realised that it's possible to share your life with someone; that it's possible to be in love and have a best friend.

What do you see when you imagine the person you'll end up with?
Just a partner in crime, really. Someone that brings out the best in me, and vice versa.

Is physical attraction an important aspect?
Well, it's the most immediate thing, of course. But on its own it's not enough. You never want to get stuck with someone who's gorgeous but can't muster up an ounce of good pillow talk.

MR LEE MULLINS & MS ADENA WALLINGFORD

Mr Mullins, 29, is the director of personal training at Bodyism, a bespoke health programme based in London's Bulgari Hotel. He met his girlfriend, the beautiful Ms Adena Wallingford, 28, while she was working at the hotel's reception. She is now PA to the director of Bodyism, Mr James Duigan. The couple, who have been dating for two years, are now engaged and live together in Notting Hill with Teddy, their dachshund puppy.

How did you meet?

LEE: I saw Adena in the lobby of the hotel. My boss introduced me as "Sexy Lee". It took me a long time to drum up the confidence to ask her out for lunch, but she said, "OK". She didn't mention that it was her birthday that day.

ADENA: At lunch, he asked me if I had any plans in the evening – I did, of course. I had a dinner planned with all of my friends, but I told him that I was free, and cancelled it.

LEE: We went out for dinner that evening, and I asked her to lunch the next day. We ended up going out four times in two days.

What do you like about each other?

LEE: She's beautiful, of course. But she also has a really attractive, friendly personality – and she's got a great laugh.

ADENA: What I liked from the start was how he wasn't scared to show his feelings. Other people might wait three days to text you back, but Lee was always open about the fact that he wanted to see me.

Where did you get your notion of love from?

ADENA: I learnt a lot from my grandparents. My grandfather was Indonesian and my grandmother was Japanese. Back then, Japanese people married Japanese people. So when they got engaged, my grandmother's family practically disowned her. Love, to me, is about sacrifice. It's being together at any cost.

LEE: I got my ideas of love mostly from Leona Lewis songs.

ADENA: Ha ha!

LEE: Just kidding. My parents have taught me a lot. They make each other laugh, and I've always loved watching their little rituals. Just little things they do every day because they love each other.

What's the secret to having a loving, happy relationship?

LEE: Always being open, sharing and talking with each other. And laughing, too.

MR TOM SLEIGH

Mr Sleigh, 35, works for Lloyds Bank, but at the time of writing is on a secondment working with Sir Richard Lambert, the ex-editor of the *Financial Times*, as part of an independent body monitoring standards across the UK banking industry. He is also an elected member of the Common Council of the City of London, a venerable local authority that represents the Square Mile (and its world-leading financial sector). Mr Sleigh has been single for two years, although he does admit that "recently, all of my dates have been with the same person".

What was your first experience of love?
I was 20, and I'd just graduated. He was beautiful – a couple of years younger than me and with the most charismatic personality. At the time, neither of us was ready to acknowledge that we were gay, but despite that, we spent all of our time together.

What prevented you from coming to terms with your sexuality?
This was a while ago – it was pre-mainstream gay characters on TV. I went to a state school; "gay" was an insult. Coming from an environment like that, you can imagine that you build up these barriers in your head. The sad consequence was that that was my first experience of love, but it took me years to realise. When he left the country, I couldn't understand the anger at the sadness that I felt – looking back, it's obvious that it was a broken heart.

Any regrets?
I should have been better at keeping in touch. But would I change it? No. I think it was an incredible experience. To have that heart-soaring excitement of being with someone, followed by that crushing feeling of losing someone, is really one of the defining emotional journeys of a person's life.

What's love?
When I picture love, I picture someone who has a really clear idea of what they want to be and what they want to achieve in life, but they're willing to do something completely different, for no other reason than that they love somebody. It's a very powerful feeling.

Isn't there an element of comfort to it, too?
I suppose so. Isn't it nice coming home, knowing there'll be someone else around, someone to care for and worry about that isn't yourself?

Are you a romantic person?
I'm romantic, but not sentimental… But I think romance is fantastic.

MR TOM WARREN

Mr Warren, 26, spent his teens and early twenties travelling the world as a model, after being scouted in Covent Garden. In late 2013 he founded Lock Studios, a photographic studio in east London. Despite his undeniably impressive credentials, he is single at the time of writing.

What's your relationship status?
My Facebook status is currently single.

Is that an accurate representation?
It's probably said that for a long time! I don't tend to declare my relationships across social media. But yes, I've been single for a while. My last relationship lasted about a year and a half. The strains and stresses of setting up your own business...

What does love mean to you?
I think that the media portrayal, the "Hollywood ideal" of love is very far from the reality. And I think there's a distinction between love and being "in love", too... I don't suppose that any couple that has spent years and years together can claim to have been "in love" the whole time. Love is more... you know that excerpt from *Captain Corelli's Mandolin*, the one that everyone reads at their wedding? I think there's a lot of truth in that.

FYI: "Love itself is what is left over when being in love has burned away".

What's the most romantic thing you've ever done?
When I was about 12, I thought I was in love. I grew up in Norfolk, where everyone lives about 45 minutes from one another. School had just finished and I thought that I wasn't going to see this girl for the whole summer, so I took my old mountain bike and cycled 17 miles to meet up with this girl and snog her. It seemed like a long way at the time. Then I cycled all the way back.

What do you think the secret is to keeping a relationship going?
Making an effort, not resting on your laurels and making time for each other. And saying "I love you" from time to time doesn't hurt, either.

MR STUART HARRISON
& MS CHRISTINE HARRISON

Mr Harrison and his wife Christine got married on 19 July 1969, at the ages of 22 and 20 years old, respectively. They live together near Skipton in North Yorkshire and have three grown-up children, the youngest of whom is none other than our very own Editor, Ms Jodie Harrison.

How did you meet?

STUART: We used to live on the same street. I'd wolf-whistle at this blonde girl who used to walk across the fairway when I was playing golf...

CHRISTINE: I couldn't stand it!

STUART: When we started to get close, we'd spend the day together – but at night I'd be back at my home, and she'd be at hers. We didn't have any way of contacting each other, so we used to turn our bedroom lights on and off. I'd switch my light on, and she'd see it and switch her light on. Then off, then back on again. This used to go on for hours...

CHRISTINE: Until we realised that we really did need to go to sleep.

STUART: It was just an acknowledgement that we were thinking about each other, I suppose. When you fall in love with someone, you want to be with them all the time.

How has your idea of love developed over the years?

STUART: When you've been with someone for such a long time you develop a bond. We'll often find each other thinking the same things. It can be quite spooky.

CHRISTINE: We're totally at ease with each other. When the kids come to stay, they'll say, "you're bickering, you're wittering". But that's just how we are. Being in love after all this time means being comfortable enough around each other that there's no tension.

What do you think has kept you going?

CHRISTINE: Well, we still fancy each other.

STUART: She's always had the most gorgeous legs. And I've always been a leg man.

CHRISTINE: You're too kind!

Do you believe in the idea that people can complete each other?

CHRISTINE: I think that one of our early mistakes was believing that your partner could provide you with everything, and that you could provide everything for them. As you develop, it's important to realise the importance of having your own time and your own friends.

STUART: I've always been more into sport than Christine, for instance. And that's good; it gives us space to do our own thing. But even now, I'll occasionally go away for a golf trip, and I find myself missing her. The truth is, we've been around each other for so long, and in love for so long, that we don't know any different.

What advice would you give the younger you?

CHRISTINE: If we knew what we know now, I think we'd have given each other more space. We were very possessive with each other when we were young.

STUART: If she ever went out with other friends, I must admit, I used to resent it. Of course, when you're young and you're passionate, that's just the way it is. Jealousy can make you realise just how much the other person means to you – but if you don't control it, it can destroy a relationship.

What's the best thing to have come out of your marriage?

CHRISTINE: Children. And being able to watch them flourish and grow.

STUART: When our first child was born, I was over the moon. I called in after work to a little jewellery shop, which made necklaces with gold letters to spell out names. We weren't well off, though, and Christine would have been very expensive. I went for Kit, instead.

CHRISTINE: It's something I still wear now.

GENTS AND THEIR SCENTS

*These icons understood that aftershave is an expression
of personality rather than a substitute for it. Here we dissect
their distinctive colognes*

Words by Mr Ahmed Zambarakji

THE PROGRESSIVE MAN may have moved beyond soap and
water but as the grooming market grows, it becomes increasingly
hard for guys to navigate. The sheer volume of new products, never
mind the convoluted Franglais/ blind-you-with-science jargon
emblazoned on every box, is bewildering. And so, with tangible
results in mind, we've separated the wheat from the chaff and
selected five essential products to help you make an impeccable
first impression.

SPECIAL NO 127 BY FLORIS
Sir Winston Churchill

It reveals a lot about Britain's heroic war-time leader that he was a fan of pretty floral fragrances. Floris, one of the most quintessential British brands, has records of the former prime minister making repeat purchases of Special No 127, a scent originally crafted in 1890 for Russia's Grand Duke Orloff that bursts with neroli, lavender and geranium. Incongruously, it was also favoured by one Ms Eva Perón.

ACQUA DI PARMA COLONIA BY ACQUA DI PARMA
Mr Cary Grant

This short-lasting citrus cologne was dabbed on the necks of
Messrs Humphrey Bogart, David Niven and Cary Grant and many
other silver-screen stars during Hollywood's Golden Age. It was
relegated to the status of cult classic in the 1960s when commercial
fragrances for men became widely available. Its recent renaissance,
courtesy of LVMH, has avoided a heartless reformulation and
the new bottle of Colonia remains true to the original recipe, from
the sparkling citric top to the lemon-infused mellow middle and
woody base.

MITSOUKO BY GUERLAIN
Sir Charles Chaplin

Sir Charles Chaplin was an infamous philanderer, which may or may not have been connected to the fact that he wore a landmark women's fragrance that has been evocatively described as "bottled porn". While that wasn't quite the intention of creator Mr Jacques Guerlain (he was aiming for an olfactory homage to romantic intrigue as described in the novel of the era, *La Bataille*, by Mr Claude Farrère), this scent is still one of the most important creations in fragrance history. Modern men who are brave enough to try Mitsouko would do well to start with the eau de toilette rather than the powerful eau de parfum formulation.

POUR HOMME BY VAN CLEEF & ARPELS
Mr Serge Gainsbourg

Were you able to make out the aftershave that lay beneath the
cloud of cigarette smoke that permanently enveloped the cabbage-
headed Monsieur Gainsbourg, you'd whiff Van Cleef's signature
fragrance for men – a heady mix of leather, moss, amber and
patchouli sprinkled with random florals that symbolises his dark
and brooding nature. As intense, sinister and complex as the man
himself, and just as likely to inspire as much wanton lust.

BOIS DU PORTUGAL BY CREED
Mr Frank Sinatra

As its name suggests this classic and grown-up fragrance is deeply woody. The effects achieved by the layers of sandalwood, cedarwood, bergamot and lavender are sophisticated and elegant, but still expressive. As such it was a perfect accompaniment to Mr Sinatra's faultlessly tailored wardrobe, and to his mature and world-weary demeanour.

THE KNACK
(AND HOW TO GET IT)

*Experts offer practical advice
on a variety of life's more unexpected,
as well as conventional, conundrums*

HOW TO PATCH A PUNCTURE

By Mr Donald Little, former bicycle courier

ELEVEN RAIN-SOAKED YEARS as a Glasgow-based cycle
messenger might not bring you any amount of financial security,
but it certainly teaches you a few invaluable lessons you wouldn't
stumble across in your average line of work – mainly, that cycling
more than 60 miles a day will bring you the sort of fitness you'll
never reach again in your life; that your loins will never quite
recover from eight hours on the saddle; that sudden death could
be around every slippery corner; and lastly, that a puncture is
an unwelcome and costly delay to your working day. The latter
teaching has had its advantages – even though I gave up the courier
game several years back, I can still fix a puncture as if my next pint
of beer depended on it. Here's how…

I

ASSESS THE DAMAGE

Have a quick look at the exterior of the tyre. If there's something obviously amiss such as a piece of glass or a nail then great – there will be no need to hunt around for a microscopic hole. If the problem is in the rear tyre, leave the wheel on the bike to save time. Otherwise, whip the wheel out of the frame, deflate it and, using your thumbs, push the tyre away from the rim all the way around on both sides. Slip the tyre lever under one edge of the tyre and then insert the second lever a few inches along. Work your way around until there is enough room to pull the inner tube out. The tyre doesn't need to come off completely, just one side will do.

2

LOCATE THE HOLE

Pumping a few strokes of air into the exposed inner tube will expand the hole, making it easier to find (it can inflate to a considerable size without danger of exploding). Run the tube past your ear, or if the traffic is noisy, wet your lips and move the tube past your mouth (I wouldn't advocate licking it unless you are really desperate). Soon enough, you should feel the escaping air blow against your lips.

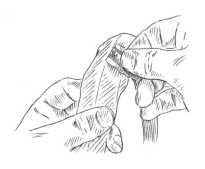

3
BUFF AND SEAL

Use the repair kit's bit of sandpaper to buff the area around the hole until the glossy finish goes. If the hole is near the moulding line, buff it flat (or shave it off with a blade), as it will stop the patch sealing effectively. If you threw the sandpaper away then use the nearest brick wall, pavement or your calves' stubble. That said, if you shave your legs for cycling yet can't fix a puncture, you need to man up.

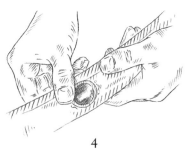

4
PATCH UP

Spread a thin and uniform amount of rubber cement around the area of the hole. Allow it to dry and become tacky (be patient) and then smooth the patch on. Press it firmly in place and give it a minute. Find the little block of chalk in your kit and scrape some on and around the patched area. This will stop it sticking to anything it shouldn't do on the way back into the tyre.

Put a little more air in the tube (making it easier to feed back into the tyre) and insert it starting at the valve. Work your way around the wheel, tucking the tube into the deepest part of the rim and ensuring it doesn't twist or get pinched. Now that the tube is in, start working the edge of the tyre (bead) back onto the rim. Starting again at the valve, push the tyre bead over the edge of the rim with your thumbs. It will get tight as you work your way around. You'll be tempted to use levers but don't – you will invariably end up pinching the tube and have to start again. Ensure the tyre is seated evenly all the way around then pump it up, pausing regularly to check the tyre for any lumps that may indicate the tube has become trapped. If all is well then pump it up to full pressure and you're good to go.

SOME COMMON MISTAKES

BEING HASTY

Make sure you locate and remove the cause of the puncture the first time around. If it's still lodged in the tyre you'll be fixing it again very shortly. If the hole is on the underside of the inner tube then check for a protruding spoke or damaged rim tape.

STAYING IN THE RAIN

Messengers from Seattle to Glasgow will tell you how miserable it is to fix a puncture in the rain. Not only does it dampen the height of your mohawk, it means the puncture patch won't stick, so save yourself time by trying to fix things under some shelter.

NEGLECTING YOUR TYRES

If there's a small rip in the sidewall of the tyre the tube will bulge through and promptly puncture. You can "bodge" a quick repair using a piece of old tyre or a few layers of gaffer tape on the inside of the tyre (during particularly lucrative phases, I used to line it using a £1 note or a dollar bill, depending on the local currency).

MISSING SOMETHING

Finally, ensure there is only one puncture (if you're unlucky enough to get one, why not two?). Sometimes you may have a "snakebite" or "pinch flat", caused when the tube is nipped between the rim and an object, leaving two holes next to each other.

HOW TO UNDRESS
IN FRONT OF A LADY

By Ms Jodie Harrison

WHILE the correct means of dressing oneself should be
a consideration for every discerning gentleman, the appropriate
method of undressing also requires discussion, particularly if your
audience is of the ever-critical female variety. It's understandable
that the throes of passion might bring about a certain degree
of sartorial nonchalance, but it's certainly no excuse for being
slapdash. Trust me, womenfolk the world over unite in this one
belief: a man should never be left standing in just a T-shirt.

1

START WITH YOUR SMALLS

No, I'm not talking about your underpants (who are you, Superman?) but details and accessories. Shoes are your first port of call simply because by approaching these first you'll ensure yourself against any stuck trouser/ tripping incidents later down the line. Then look to your socks, making sure you store them safely in your shoes. And, no, Mr Randy Newman was wrong about the hat thing – you cannot leave your hat on (but well done for wearing one).

2

TOP TO TOE

It's important to start from the top and work your way down. Remove your coat or jacket followed by your tie and shirt or T-shirt. If your sleeves are rolled up then try to unroll them, as this will save on added creasing should you need to reuse your shirt for the "walk of shame" home. If your watch is a Rolex, keep it on. She will no doubt approve of your attention to detail.

3
THE SERIOUS PART

Your trousers should be removed with some measured haste – why stall things at this stage? It's probably ideal if you do the first part (unfastening) standing up (let her attempt this), and the last part (kicking them off) sitting down. This will save on any mood-killing, stumbling mishaps.

4
THE LAST LEAP

The "pants" issue is something we women talk about more than men probably like to imagine. Underpants, like cars, tell us everything we need to know about the man inside them. I have often heard female friends cite a man's poor taste in underwear as something of a date-night dealbreaker, so take note and take care when choosing them. Keep them neat, plain and clean – cartoons or giggle-inducing patterns have no place in your trousers. When it comes to removing them, leave it till the time seems right.

SOME COMMON MISTAKES

DOWN TO A T

Whether you're unpeeling in front of someone new or someone familiar, there can be no excuse for the brain-searing image of a grown man left standing in just a T-shirt. It evokes disturbing similarities to semi-naked toddlers on a beach. Do yourself a favour: take the T-shirt off first, not last.

DANCING

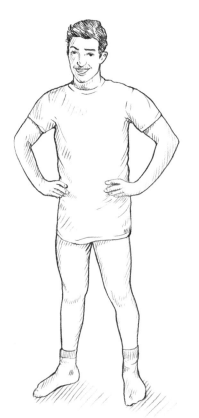

Women may be able to carry off the odd alluring wiggle or pivot thanks to their innate curves and slinkiness. Men cannot. Don't even think about it.

SOCKS

Like your T-shirt, these should be addressed pretty early on in the proceedings. Girls look sexy in just a pair of socks (who can forget those American Apparel adverts?). Men on the other hand? Hmmm, not so much.

HOW TO REMEMBER
PEOPLE'S NAMES

By Ms Jodie Harrison

YOU KNOW HOW IT GOES; you recognise the face as they approach you at a party, your brain scans and searches for context, history, and above all, a name. But, more often than not, it doesn't come and you are left standing there like a bumbling fool. Forgetting or mixing up a name is one of life's cheek-flushers, but as business coach and author of *How to Win Friends and Influence People* Mr Dale Carnegie once explained, "A person's name is to him or her the sweetest and most important sound in any language" so it really is best avoided. Here, we show you how to play the name game... and win.

1
MAKE THE DECISION

One of the major steps to remembering people's names is actually making the effort to do so. It's very easy to proclaim yourself a name vacuum and never trying to improve your memory, but by making the commitment, you can get better at it. It's certainly something the Californian speechcoach Mr Chris Witt advises: "Before going to a meeting or a party or anywhere you might meet people, remind yourself of your commitment. And recommit yourself: 'I will make my best effort to remember the names of the people I meet.'"

2
HEAR THEM OUT

When you are being introduced to someone, listen to them and look them in the eye. After the intro, repeat their name out loud a few times to set it in your mind. It often helps to ask them about their name, such as, "Did I pronounce that correctly?" or "____ is an interesting name, where is it from?" It goes without saying that this should only be applied to interesting names. No one needs to know the phonetics behind the name "Dave". You'll just sound condescending, not to mention odd.

3
IMAGINE THAT

As the brain remembers images much better than it remembers words, try paying close attention to any notable physical features during the introduction. While you chat, it also helps to associate their name with something visual. For example, should the person in question be called Helen Hammond, imagine her head as a big side of ham (and no, we are not joking). If their names don't instantly muster up images, panic not, by just attempting to correlate their name with something physical you will have made a mental impression.

4
TAKE NOTE

In the age of the ever-expanding Apple cart, there can be no excuse not to take note of a new name on your iPhone should you believe the person to be someone you might meet again. It's wise to do this after the event rather than during your first conversation. Nothing screams "serial killer" more than looking as if you are taking down someone's characteristics within the first two minutes of meeting them.

5
SWAP DETAILS

If the meeting is business related, ask for a card and scribble down details of the event you met at on the back. People love handing out cards, especially when they have gone to the trouble of spending several hours designing and ordering them. If all this sounds like a lot of work, that's exactly the point. Remembering someone's name will make people feel important, memorable and, in turn, more receptive to you, opening up a few doors along the way.

SOME COMMON MISTAKES

STARING AND SCARING

While we advise taking note of features, we also advise keeping it discreet. Being remembered is nice, but not when you are being remembered for being a weirdo.

OVER AND OUT

Repeating the person's name during a conversation can be an integral part of committing it to memory, but don't overdo it. People like hearing their own name, but one too many times can be peculiar.

LEAVING IT HANGING

If you are faced with the tricky situation of introducing your friend to your sadly unmemorable acquaintance, introduce the friend first, "This is my partner, Frank". If Frank is any sort of friend he'll then reach forward, shake their hand and ask their name, alleviating you of your embarrassment.

FORGETTING

Sometimes, there's just no getting away from the fact that you have forgotten someone's name. In these circumstances we advocate the following: "Darling, meet darling."

HOW TO ROAST A LAMB

By Mr Tim Hayward, writer, broadcaster and author of
Food DIY: How to Make Your Own Everything

RAISE THE STAKES in terms of outdoor cooking by roasting an entire lamb over an open fire. Providing enough meat to feed 40 people, it creates an impressive spectacle and gives ample opportunity to stand around with friends and drink cold beer.

I
POLE POSITION

Choose a scaffolding pole about twice the length of your lamb. At the midpoint, drill a hole through it big enough to thread a piece of reinforcing bar through. Drill two more holes about 50cm either side. At 10cm in from each end, drill two more holes, at right angles to each other, through the spit. Thread the pole up through the middle of your lamb, through the mouth, if it still has its head on, and out beneath the tail. Place the animal in the middle of the pole. Take three pieces of reinforcing bar, about 50cm each in length, and poke them horizontally through the carcass, through the holes in the pole and back out through the other side. At this stage, while the inside of the carcass is still accessible, season it liberally.

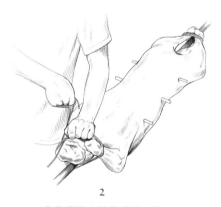

2

LOCK AND LOAD

You'll need to restrain the carcass into a tubular shape to make the cooking even, so either tuck up the legs and wire them into position or wrap the whole carcass in chicken wire and stitch it closed with a lighter gauge of steel wire. Keep two extra pieces of reinforcing bar handy. By inserting them into the holes at the ends of the spit you can rotate the whole thing or lock it into place.

3
STEP CHANGE

Dig a V-shaped trench four paving slabs long and line it with two runs of slabs at a diagonal to each other. Now lay in the last four slabs horizontally. This creates a fire bed with ventilation beneath and two reflecting panels that concentrate the heat on the meat. Clear a patch of ground near to the spit where you can start a second fire to keep up your supply of coals during cooking. Erect the two stepladders at either end of the fire pit, well back from the heat with their steps facing inwards. The steps will enable you to adjust the height of the spit.

Pour a couple of bags of charcoal into the pit and light it. You can use a chimney to start the fire at three or four points along the length, or a blowtorch. Always work in the same direction along the pit so that the heat will remain constant when you refuel. Once the coals have a covering of white ash and are glowing fiercely, bring the spit into position and prop it on the steps of the ladders, using the reinforcing bars to lock it in position.

4
SPIT ROTATION

Rotate the spit regularly to achieve even browning and carefully extinguish any flare-ups caused by dripping fat. A cup of water usually does the job.

Half an hour into cooking, start to pour a bag of charcoal onto the cleared patch of ground and light it. Once it's glowing, shovel it into the fire pit to keep the heat steady and start another bag burning for the refuel.

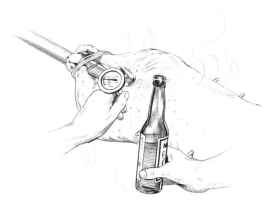

5
SWEET AND LOW

Once the outside of the animal is browned and the fat is beginning to melt and flow, you can lower the cooking temperature by raising the spit a little or by reducing the amount of charcoal in each refuel. If you can only place your hand above the coals for three seconds, you're at the right temperature.

Now it's just a matter of refuelling, turning, drinking beer and being patient. Use a probe thermometer to check internal temperatures and after about an hour or so you should be able to make a reasonable estimate of your finishing time.

6

REST AND RELAX

Once the internal temperature of the meat at the thickest point (usually in the muscle at the top of the leg) reaches 75°C, lift the spit off, have a couple of hungry assistants move the ladders to somewhere quiet, away from the fire, and then replace the spit on the ladders so the meat can rest. Half an hour or 45 minutes is not an unreasonable time to rest a whole lamb. It will retain its heat, but keep rotating the spit during resting as it helps to redistribute the fat and juices.

To serve, simply lop or tear off great lumps and eat with salad, bread and cold beer. The main point of food like this is to rip into it in a kind of feeding frenzy. Nice for a family barbecue, particularly if your family are half-starved Viking raiders.

YOU'LL NEED

A length of scaffolding pole	Several bags of barbecue charcoal
Some wire	A shovel
A dozen cheap concrete paving slabs	A few lengths of reinforcing bar
Two stepladders	Oh… and a lamb

SOME COMMON MISTAKES

NOT ALLOWING ENOUGH TIME

If you're cooking lunch for a hundred hungry people at a wedding reception and it takes all afternoon you'll be very unpopular.

FAILING TO RESTRAIN THE ANIMAL

If the carcass is not properly wired onto the frame then all the meat will fall off and you'll have to grub around in the ashes looking for the flesh.

SCARING YOUR GUESTS

Leaving the head on the animal can freak some people out.

FOOTWEAR FAUX PAS

Don't wear flip-flops or espadrilles. You're cooking 75lbs of animal and it's full of fat, some of which may drip onto your ankles. Wear some sensible shoes.

HOW TO DRESS FOR A PARTY

By Mr Tom Stubbs

"AND WHAT COSTUME shall the poor girl wear to all tomorrow's parties?" droned Nico in the Velvet Underground's famous song. Although the subject of "what outfit" is commonly associated with the fairer sex, it is also a pressing question for men. Any social event is an excuse to crank up the style in a near-competitive manner, but in particular a party presents a man with the opportunity to display his style savvy. Given the romantic rewards on offer at any good party the manner in which you dress, and how far you take it, are critical. The challenge is to find the path between looking as if you are trying too hard, and looking undistinguished. Here's how to walk that line.

I
PLAN YOUR OUTFIT

Use our dress-code guide to gauge the necessary level of formality. Then, in a spirit of optimism, consider the location, imagine the mood, and the kind of impression you want to make.

2
APPLY SOME PRACTICAL CONSIDERATIONS

Will the other guests be coming straight from work? Is there going to be a cloakroom, or are you going to have to dance wearing your coat? Is spaghetti being served at dinner (in which case you may want to wear a bow tie rather than a necktie – shirts are easier to clean than ties)?

3
POP YOUR COLLAR

Bear in mind that the style of your shirt collar is a very potent element of a suit-based outfit. Consider penny collars, spread collars, tab collars, or even using a collar pin, to focus attention on your tie knot. Equally, if you're going tieless you may need a button down, or a starched collar, to stop the shirt collar collapsing under the jacket.

4
MIX IT UP

If the dress code is open to interpretation dress down a dinner jacket with some casual elements (Mr Bryan Ferry once wore a denim shirt under his tux), such as a rollneck or velvet slippers. Alternatively, you could wear a Marcella shirt with dark jeans and highly polished loafers.

5
IT'S PRETTY BLACK AND WHITE

For an evening look that's understated and sharp, save the splashes of colour for daywear, and instead create an outfit based around a black or midnight-blue suit, a crisp white shirt and a pair of elegant shoes. The only eye-catching accessory a man needs is a good-looking woman on his arm.

6
WHEN IN DOUBT...

At a complete loss because your host can't come up with a dress code? Then try wearing a pair of eye-catching shoes or slippers, with a dark pair of neat jeans and a pale blue shirt. Examples include ponyskin or embroidered slippers, highly polished dark blue, claret or green loafers or Oxfords, and polished ankle boots.

LOUNGE SUIT

This calls for a regular suit. The trousers and jacket should match, whether they're made of tweed, flannel or mohair, but smooth fabric is best. A shirt and tie are highly recommended, but a slim polo neck can work.

SMART / CASUAL

This suggests the hosts can't make up their mind on the dress code. We suggest a pair of chinos, loafers (or sneakers if the emphasis is on the casual), a shirt and a blazer.

COCKTAIL

The ideal answer is a cocktail suit, which will be dark, lean and have a slight sheen. However, velvet jackets are also appropriate, and jewellery is an acceptable accessory.

BLACK TIE

If it's a private party a dark-coloured velvet jacket worn with black trousers is a good option, while a midnight-blue evening suit is always a stylish choice.

WHITE TIE

This involves a tailcoat and a white waistcoat – it doesn't just mean wearing a white bow tie with a dinner jacket. But as this dress code is usually reserved for state occasions and ambassadorial receptions, if you receive white tie invitations you probably don't need me to explain how to do it.

HOW TO SURVIVE WHEN
LOST AT SEA

By Mr Steve Callahan, sailor, survivor and
author of Adrift: 76 Days Lost at Sea

MOST MEN have what I call the "exploratory gene", a drive within them to go beyond their comfort zone and get back to nature. These experiences have a risk associated with them, and I learnt this the hard way when in 1982 my boat hit something (I believe it was a whale) and sank. I was lost adrift for 76 days in a 6ft life raft. Since then, I've interviewed other survivors and a commonality among us is that, while none of us would like to go through the experience again, we all gained a great deal from it. It sounds clichéd but there is a truth to the notion that by enduring such horror, we find out that we are much hardier than we thought we could be. In my case, one of the most enlightening elements was learning about my great weaknesses. As your life drags before your eyes like a bad B-grade movie, you see your failures, but that realisation gives you a purpose – come out of it, rectify those shortcomings, realign your priorities and move on. Men need experiences where they become the insignificant factor to do that. Should you be unlucky enough to be stranded at sea, here are a few pointers that might make the situation seem a little better.

I
BE PREPARED

I mean this in both a psychological and physical sense. No man should just jump into a situation without having the proper experience leading up to it. Sail overnight, do passages and understand that whatever can go wrong will go wrong and even whatever can't go wrong will still go wrong. If you are properly prepared, you can get used to dealing with crises and problems in steps.

2
THE SMALLER PICTURE

Don't get overwhelmed by what might seem like an epic, endless journey with an unachievable goal. When lost at sea, you have to forget about your wants and focus on your needs. In my case that was a) keeping the raft together; if it wasn't afloat I wouldn't survive, and b) collecting water and hunting for food; you can live a week without water and maybe a month without food, so water was the priority. Keep things in perspective.

3
TAKE A RADIO

My experience happened in what feels like the Stone Age in terms of the equipment I had; an emergency radio only monitored by aircraft within 250 miles. Now everything is monitored by satellite. I had flares and saw ships within two weeks, but the chances of anyone seeing a flare are slim. The chances of someone being on the other end of a radio are much better. If I'd had a hand-held VHF radio, I probably would have been picked up in the first two weeks or so.

4
FOOD FOR THOUGHT

Fish heads, guts and raw seagull may seem disgusting at first, but after a couple of weeks of no food, even the weirdest things became appealing. As I starved, my psychology changed towards food. My body craved fats and sugars, things that were found in the guts and organs of fish; fish eyes were soup, liver was dessert. The parts I now cringe at were, at the time, delicious. Don't freak out and starve yourself.

5
KEEP BUSY

In the same way your body needs water and food to survive, your mind needs to keep working to make it. In these situations, a lot of people die a week or two before they should. Their bodies could keep going but they just give up. Set yourself daily tasks, reward yourself with a small ration of water and keep plugging away. Every little step you take adds up to the big reward at the end: getting found and surviving.

6
DON'T GO TO SEA

This is a simple yet effective preventative method although sadly, it's not one I'm capable of doing. All men have a need for security and comfort but battling that is a need for adventure and risk. For me, that's going to sea.

SOME COMMON MISTAKES

JUMPING TOO EARLY

There's a saying in the sailing world that you should always step up to your life raft. A lot of people will be tempted to get off the boat when it's stormy and scary, but I guarantee it will be 10 times worse on a life raft. Don't abandon your boat until you know it's really done for.

DRINKING UP

It's the classic error: while drinking sea water will relieve you in the short term, it will be the death of you in the long term. Don't do it. Salt water has higher salt content than your cells, so draws fluid out.

TOO MUCH, TOO SOON

You have to remember that you are in an isolated environment with limited resources; once something is gone, it's gone. If you patch a hole in the raft using a piece of cushion, that cushion currency is used up. I could have relieved my salt water sores using the medical resources I had but I knew I needed to save them in case I incurred a more serious injury. Use what you have wisely.

LOSING HOPE

It might feel as if you are trying to reach an unreachable goal but you have to stay positive, keep busy and focus on the positive. My time lost at sea enabled me to see incredible things that I would not have encountered in any other situation: the star-filled sky (there's no bigger sky country than the middle of the ocean), the shimmering bio-luminescent fish at night as they followed or were disturbed by the raft. I've talked to survivors who actually miss their experiences... there's a purity to it you'll never go through again.

BECOMING FISH BAIT

If you are lost in the Pacific, sharks will be a problem. I wasn't, but still came into contact with a few. If it happens, keep calm and keep off the bottom of the raft because if anything is poking down they will grab onto it. Like most predators, they want to avoid an injury so they will bump the boat a few times to see if you fight back. If they do this you need to show them you can hurt them. Whack it or poke it with something, anything to show you mean business.

HOW TO BATTLE BALDNESS

By Mr Philip Kingsley, trichologist*

PEOPLE SAY that it doesn't matter if a man goes bald, but it matters to him. Hair is a key factor in one's psychology and I'd be terrified if mine started to fall out, so I understand why men want to come and see me if they've got some hair loss.

I'm not a miracle worker and I can't make hair grow back, but I can keep what hair you've got, and make it look better. The least I can do is slow down hair loss; the best is maintain the quantity. Certain things will make hair grow again, but the side effects are ridiculous, dangerous, and you get a loss of libido.

I put people on a programme according to their hair's needs, and men usually do what I ask because they don't want to lose their hair. But there's no magic; you have to eat better, take the supplements and follow the programme – it's the whole caboodle that helps.

*fancy talk for a hair expert

I

TAKE CARE OF YOUR SCALP

The scalp likes to be clean, and we have proof that a flaky, itchy scalp causes hair to fall out. Everyone's scalp has flora – bacteria – and that's normal, but if something changes the scalp's balance, and the bacteria flourish, the skin will itch and flake, and that will cause the hair to fall out. We make topical treatments for the scalp.

2

HAVE SOMEONE CHECK YOUR BLOOD LEVELS

In many instances we send men for blood tests, because there may be a metabolic reason why they're having hair problems. A test might come back with everything in the normal range, but not necessarily the normal range for hair. If they need something that I can't prescribe, I send them to their doctor.

3

EAT THE RIGHT THINGS

The right thing is protein, because hair's made of protein. Many men don't eat enough protein, especially at breakfast. The best things are kippers, and the easiest are eggs – the protein is in the white – or a couple of slices of ham. I also take supplements, for vitamin B12 and zinc, and avoid too much salt and animal fat.

4
WASH IT EVERY DAY

If you saw how dirty hair is 24 hours after it's been washed you'd be horrified. But if you shampoo it and see it come out then you don't want to wash it again, so you leave it a week and then a lot more comes out. However, there's no doubt that washing it frequently, preferably daily, is better for your hair and less falls out overall.

5
USE THE RIGHT HAIR PRODUCTS

My shampoos are specific for different types of hair, and are specific for the state of the scalp. They've all been clinically tested for at least two years. Some of the lotions are for cleansing flaky scalps, some are stimulating if there's hair loss, and some are astringent.

HOW TO SCORE A DATE

By Mr Alex Chubb of The London School of Attraction

THAT UNFEASIBLY GORGEOUS BLONDE standing at the bar might look intimidating and unapproachable, but scoring a date with her is easier than it looks. It's natural to feel a little nervous, but this isn't a cold-call sales pitch. What you're offering is what every girl dreams of: to be swept off her feet on an exciting date by a cool, confident gentleman. All you have to do is follow this sequence and you'll be exchanging phone numbers and, hopefully, dinner plans.

I

THE BASICS

Make sure you're well-dressed: a man in a suit will always turn heads in a bar, but any style can work if it fits with your identity. Make sure you're well-groomed: whether you wear a moustache, stubble or full whiskers, ensure your facial hair is trimmed and soft. Remember your manners: remove your hat when you enter the bar and help the lady with her coat if you leave together.

2

THE APPROACH

Many gentlemen take the safe option when approaching a lady, but now is the time to be bold. Don't pussyfoot around asking her opinion or commenting on what she's drinking; be honest and authentic. Tell her she's caught your eye and that you wanted to meet her. When you give your compliment, make sure you focus on the person and not the object: "You look amazing in that dress," rather than, "I love your dress." It doesn't have to be a cheesy, grimace-laden exchange.

3
SEED THE DATE

Many gentlemen take the safe option when approaching a lady. "Seeding" the date is a very powerful (if a little sneaky) technique: early in the conversation, drop hints about the next time you and the girl can meet. It's a lot easier to get her number if you've already made allusions to seeing her again. Try to make this as organic as possible. If you buy her a drink, tell her she can get the first one "the next time I see you".

4
SELL THE DATE

Only a man with little ambition and even less imagination will propose seeing a lady again "for another drink". It is your job as a man to sell the date. Mention the "great atmosphere" in a cocktail bar, the "amazing cakes" in your favourite patisserie or the beauty of a walk by the river. Promise excitement and adventure.

5

CLOSE

Never ask for the number in isolation. "Please may I have your number?" will only trigger a tacit (or audible) "Why?" from the lady. Always exchange details to facilitate seeing each other again. If you have been seeding and selling a trip to the pictures, that's your justification to close: "Let me know your number and I'll call you on Friday to arrange." It would be a hard-hearted lady indeed who didn't agree at this stage!

SOME COMMON MISTAKES

NOT APPROACHING HER

It's all too easy to listen to those negative thoughts and excuses, but don't take yourself out of the game before it has even begun. Remember Mr Woody Allen's infamous quote: "Eighty per cent of success is just showing up."

ASKING TOO MANY QUESTIONS

Once you've approached, it's your job to draw her into the conversation before expecting her to answer your questions. Stick to statements, observations and stories until she shows interest.

BEING TOO AGREEABLE

If she's really beautiful, you'll feel an overwhelming urge to agree with everything she says. Resist! You'll gain more Brownie points by showing that you have your own values and opinions.

HOW TO CHOOSE THE RIGHT SUIT

By Mr Toby Bateman

A SUIT IS A SERIOUS INVESTMENT, and as such should be treated with a certain degree of po-facedness. The starting point when choosing a new suit is to be clear about its purpose. This may sound obvious enough, I know, but these things are no longer as straightforward as they once were. Nowadays, the suit has many potential uses: to wear to the office, wedding participation, court attendance, at the horse races, partying, front man of a new band – the list is almost endless. Whatever the purpose, the most important thing to remember is that you should always look better with a suit on than without it. That's the whole point. It hides the bits of your body you would rather not flaunt and emphasises those you would. That's why the ladies always appreciate a guy in a good suit. Here, I've outlined how the suit can work for any situation, professional or otherwise.

I

THE BANKER/ LAWYER

Serious work requires a serious suit. Consequently, you should keep it pretty safe when it comes to colour, pattern and fit. This may or may not involve a tie (although in my opinion it should and I fully support the recent resurgence in this "proper" way of completing your office outfit). Try to stick to a classical structure in a dark base colour that is cut to fit – it should not swathe you in fabric nor wrap you up like clingfilm. Solid navy blues and greys, from charcoal to mid-grey, are the most versatile. Add individuality through details – perhaps a knitted tie, pocket square or colourful socks.

2
THE ARCHITECT/ DESIGNER

Lucky you – you can afford to go a little more off-piste. A suit in this situation could very acceptably be worn without a tie, or with a T-shirt or fine-gauge crew-neck sweater and a pair of sneakers, if the suit fabric and fit is right. Take a classic colour such as navy or light grey, pick less formal fabrications such as cotton or linen (these often come half-lined and unstructured to fit closer to the actual shoulder shape, with a slimmer cut sleeve), opt for a shorter-cut jacket and slim-cut trousers that finish right on top of the shoe without a break – this way the sneaker won't look wrong.

3
THE WEDDING-GOER

Whether guest or groom, remember that the photos are destined to haunt you for a long time. So, unless you are Sir Mick Jagger, err on the side of caution. If you are eschewing a classic morning suit (or tuxedo) then I would advise a one- or two-button single-breasted wool or mohair suit, in blue or grey, with a slim but not skinny cut, a classic shoe, a plain white shirt (which all photograph well), and a tie and pocket square according to what makes you feel good and which express a little about yourself. As a groom, avoid trying to match the bridesmaids – you are, after all, your own man.

A FEW EXTRA THINGS TO CONSIDER

THE SHAPE

Single-breasted, two-button suits are still the default, but a one-button version can add dressiness. If you really want to "power dress", adding a waistcoat to your suit will ensure no one questions a word you say. Double-breasting is definitely back on the scene and, right now, is a frequent sight here at the MR PORTER offices. As a rule of thumb, the lapel width on your jacket should mirror the width of your tie.

THE FIT

Go for something as slim as you can afford without it being tight. Jacket lengths have been getting shorter over recent years – anything with a centre back length of between 72cm and 75cm would be considered on-trend. Trousers are still mostly worn straight, slim and not too long (err on the shorter side when your tailor is pinning them – people will take this as being very European). Italians would not be seen dead in trousers that touch their shoes.

FABRIC AND PATTERN

Plain suits are more interesting if they have some fabric texture. Broken twills, herringbone, tweed – these are the details to look for. Blends are important – a mohair and wool mix will give a slight sheen (not shine) and crispness that look sharp. Linen or cotton will soften the formality and make a T-shirt wearable with the outfit. Regarding patterns, checks are currently more important than stripes – a Prince of Wales check is very acceptable.

HOW TO ACE
A SKYPE INTERVIEW

By Mr Henry Farrar-Hockley

THE TRADITIONAL ritual of an *Apprentice*-style grilling in a meeting room is edging closer to retirement. Video interviews are a growth trend, with six in 10 recruiters now switching on their webcams, cutting time and cost for both sides and removing the need to turn up at all – in the flesh, at least. And given that 93% of human communication is non-verbal, it's not hard to see why virtual interviewees take precedence over conventional phoners.

Of course, there's a knack to proving your worth to a potential employer from the comfort of your own house. Which is why we Skyped four experts in the field to help keep you in the frame.

1
BRING YOURSELF
UP TO SPEED

Your stellar performance will be wasted if your broadband is not up to it. Connection speeds can be hindered by everything from location to time of day and your router's firmware – not to mention others hogging the Wi-Fi. Carry out a speed check at speedtest.net; Skype recommends a minimum bandwidth of 1.5Mbps for a broadcast-worthy HD video call. Avoid smartphones – your interview will end up looking like one long selfie.

2
SET THE SCENE

Unlike at a conventional face-to-face summit, your interrogator can only focus on your webcam's field of view. "Your environment should resemble a working space," advises Mr James Peters, head of recruitment at Hailo. "I've witnessed someone do an interview from their bedroom – I'm not entirely sure what that says about them." Always test your camera and microphone before the call to ensure the picture and volume settings are correct. "Practising for a Skype interview will also have an impact on your confidence," says Dr Stephen Fletcher, director of The Occupational Psychology Centre. "As will imagining yourself being successful."

GET INTO THE ZONE

One of the biggest risks of being interviewed at home is not being in the right frame of mind, what with your TV, games console and fridge within arm's reach. "Go out for a short walk to replicate the feeling of travelling to the interview," Dr Fletcher advises. "Being online 10-15 minutes early also helps you focus; drifting in a couple of minutes beforehand will only add to your stress levels." Should your interview be with an international employer, adjust your timetable. "If it's at an unusual hour because of the time difference, get up early so you're mentally awake," he continues. Clear your diary and shut yourself away to minimise interruptions from inquisitive pets. "People also forget to turn off their mobiles," says Mr Mark Soden, a partner at Boyden Global Executive Search. "It can upset the flow, even if they're just silencing an incoming call."

4

MASTER VIRTUAL EYE CONTACT
AND BODY LANGUAGE

"On Skype you get a good insight of a person pretty quickly from their body language," Mr Peters points out. Mr Soden agrees: "You can always get a sense of what kind of a person they are from their general demeanour. Are they fidgety or relaxed, articulate or shy? At senior management level it's more about the personality fit than career experience, so this makes it all the more important to see how the candidate behaves on screen." Eye contact is also key to establishing rapport; by positioning the video window next to the webcam lens you can see your interviewer and look them straight in the eye. "Sitting slightly forward with your arms open shows engagement with your intervicwer," Dr Fletcher advises. "Don't be laid-back – in either sense – that could be misinterpreted as disinterest in the interview."

5

KEEP IT SIMPLE

Getting the aesthetics of your Skype interview right is important. "Because of the way video is encoded, the more complex the image the harder your computer will have to work to process it," explains Mr Sean Wilkes, solutions consultant at Invenias executive search software, "so don't wear striped or patterned shirts, and avoid textured walls, which will require more bandwidth to compensate." With this in mind, MR PORTER advocates the clean-cut elegance of a slim-fit Boglioli woven wool blazer with a white Burberry Brit cotton Oxford shirt for the perfect interview look. Last but not least, poor lighting could prove as off-putting as a plaid jacket; don't position yourself near windows or other strong light sources as these can obscure your face, and no employer will want to spend the best part of an hour talking to your silhouette.

THE GREAT UNKNOWN

*Mountain guides Messrs Anthony Franklin and Fred Deffey
show how best to dress for the slopes*

Words by Mr Chris Elvidge

ACCORDING TO OUR GUIDE, it's known as *une mer de nuages* –
a sea of clouds. When it forms in valleys, the surrounding peaks
pierce the surface and emerge like islands. Above this majestic
landscape, the blue sky stretches out indefinitely.

This is Mr Anthony Franklin's world. A mountain guide of some
15 years, he spends 100 days a year roaming the Alps, traversing
glaciers and mountaintops in pursuit of the finest off-piste skiing.
He lives a nomadic lifestyle during the ski season; his clients, who
meet him in Geneva, often arrive with little idea of where they are
being taken. "We could be heli-skiing in the mountains around
Courmayeur one week and glacier skiing across the border the
next. We follow the snow," he explains.

That search took MR PORTER to La Grave, a small Alpine
resort surrounded by steep, unmarked routes that has become
a Mecca for off-piste skiers. Somewhat unsurprisingly, it's also
the place that Mr Franklin calls home. Taking the resort's solitary
ski lift, we headed up through the clouds to emerge at the Col des
Ruillans at an altitude of 3,200m. Here, Mr Franklin and fellow
guide Mr Fred Deffey modelled a series of looks that mixed casual
knitwear with technical ski gear – a style that paid homage to
a more elegant era, while still remaining decidedly modern.

JAZZ ICONS

*A closer look at the enduring music and style of some
of the world's most gifted jazz musicians*

Words by Mr G Bruce Boyer

"I USED TO SEE all these great musicians," Rollins said. "There
was Coleman Hawkins, and his Cadillac and those wonderful
suits he wore. Just standing on the corner, I could see Duke
Ellington, Andy Kirk, Don Redman, Benny Carter, Sid Catlett,
Jimmy Crawford, Charlie Shavers, Al Hall, Denzil Best, and all
these kinds of men. Those guys commanded respect in the way
they carried themselves. You knew something was very true when
you saw Coleman Hawkins or any of these people. They were not
pretending."
Mr Stanley Crouch on Mr Sonny Rollins, *The New Yorker*,
9 May 2005, p66

The great classic jazz musicians were very conscious and
reflective about the way they dressed, not only because it was an
outward sign of success, but because they knew they were cultural
heroes. They represented elegance, skill and creativity in their
attitude and deportment as well as their technical virtuosity.
Some of these musicians dressed so distinctively, they influenced
fashions for generations of young men, creating a style legacy
almost as important as their musical one.

Mr Duke Ellington, France, 1960

In the thousands of gigs he and his band played, Mr Duke Ellington was royalty in every sense of the word but birthright. His band members were immaculately clothed and Mr Ellington sometimes wore white tie and tails, just to let his audience know he was as sophisticated and elegant as anyone on the silver screen. Mr Ellington designed his own shoes and ordered them in every colour and leather imaginable. He favoured suits and sports jackets in bright checks tailored drape-style by Anderson & Sheppard as well as Ivy-style ones from J. Press. He was Mr Smooth & Elegant.

Mr Coleman Hawkins, US, 1953

Mr Coleman Hawkins played with them all, from Ms Bessie Smith and Mr Louis Armstrong in the 1920s, to Messrs Ellington, Thelonious Monk and Sonny Rollins in the 1950s and 1960s. Critics said that Mr Hawkins made the tenor sax a solo instrument in jazz, and it's easy to see why. Besides his incredible technical virtuosity and a great ebullient sound, he had the *authority* of his personality. The Hawk favoured Savile Row double-breasted striped suits, white shirts with long collars and neat ties, and a blocked hat. He was an urbane commander of the realm and the ladies loved him.

Mr Dizzy Gillespie, US, 1958

Mr Dizzy Gillespie, great bop trumpeter and composer, took the hipster thing a bit beyond, and became the most visible icon of the 1940s and early 1950s Beat movement. With his heavy black-framed glasses and black beret, zoot suits complete with snake chain, thick-soled shoes and large bow ties, Mr Gillespie was the coolest cat who ever lived. He set the model that would be initially taken up by jazz musicians and their followers from the mid-1940s until Mr Miles Davis decreed the hipster look dead in 1955.

Mr Billy Eckstine, US, 1958

Mr Billy Eckstine, for whom the phrase "tall, dark and handsome" must surely have been coined, started off as a progressive jazz musician and ended up as one of the most romantic crooners of his generation. Along the way, he developed a sophisticated, less extreme version of the zoot suit the other cats in the band were wearing. Mr Eckstine's look was accentuated by a soft-but-high-rolled collar – so popular it became known as a "Mr B" – worn with skinny silk knit ties and gabardine drape-cut suits. The very model of the hip gentleman.

Mr Lester Young, UK, 1953

Mr Lester Young was Mr Hawkins' opposite in every way but
genius. While Mr Hawkins' sound commanded you to listen,
Mr Young's enticed you as it floated by. Mr Hawkins was brash and
competitive; Mr Young was shy and reticent. Mr Young preferred
zoot suits – colourful high-waisted trousers with wide legs and
pegged bottoms – long coats with wide shoulders, wide-brimmed
pork pie hats and pointy shoes with Cuban heels in colours to
match his suits. He was the consummate hipster, and his style was
evoked by Ms Billie Holiday in "Fine and Mellow".

Mr Miles Davis, US, 1958

Mr Miles Davis grew up in the shadow of Messrs Gillespie, Charlie "Bird" Parker, Monk and the other boppers, but he was very definitely his own man and had the courage of both his convictions and his taste. As good-looking as Mr Eckstine, and with the sensibility to be ahead of the curve, he dropped the bopper look at the 1955 Newport Jazz Festival when he strolled onstage wearing an Ivy-style seersucker jacket, button-down shirt and flat-front narrow trousers, all bought from Mr Charlie Davidson's Andover Shop in Massachusetts. The zoot was dead, long live jivey Ivy.

Mr Chet Baker, US, 1974

Sensually exquisite trumpeter and singer Mr Chet Baker, who made the transition away from the zoot about the same time Mr Davis did, looked like Mr James Dean and discovered the laid-back Southern California lifestyle when he moved there as a youth. When he came east to play he took up Ivy too, but he always returned to those SoCal roots; the post-war mix of sports clothes and prole gear that combined T-shirts and khakis, tennis shoes, baggy sweaters, wheat jeans, printed sports shirts and leisure jackets.

STYLE FOR SOLDIERS

Six injured servicemen tell MR PORTER *about how
a shirtmaker came to the rescue*

Words by Mr Chris Elvidge

HEADLEY COURT, the medical rehabilitation centre for the British Armed Forces, is where soldiers who have suffered severe injuries in the line of duty take the first difficult steps towards a new life. For many of these young men – some of who have lost one, two, or even three limbs – it is a life that has been altered beyond all recognition.

Supporting them along the path to recovery is a full-time team of medical officers, personal trainers, therapists and prosthetics specialists whose goal, if not to return these injured soldiers to active duty as soon as possible, is to prepare them for a transition out of the military and back into civilian life. One woman helping to ease this transition is Ms Emma Willis, who since 2008 has provided bespoke shirts for the patients of Headley Court through her charitable incentive, Style For Soldiers. A shirtmaker by trade – Ms Willis has a shop on London's Jermyn Street and a workshop in Gloucester, and her eponymous brand is available on MR PORTER – she was motivated to offer her services after hearing about the rehabilitation centre on a radio show. "I was moved to tears by their courage. I decided to visit so that I could measure these young men for a shirt as a gift to thank them for their sacrifice." Bespoke in the truest sense of the word, the finished products are often adapted to account for the soldiers' injuries, with details such as Velcro cuffs hidden by sewn-in enamel cufflinks.

What began as just shirts quickly evolved after Ms Willis realised how many of these men relied on walking sticks after their discharge from Headley Court. With a nod to the grand old military tradition of keeping up appearances, she designed a shiny black ebony cane with a buffalo horn handle and a silver band engraved with the owner's initials and regimental badge. "We've made hundreds of these now," she says. "They look more like a fashion accessory than a medical aid, and they show the world how these men sustained their injuries." And if gratitude is a measure of success, then Style For Soldiers has surely made a difference. Ms Willis' website keeps a catalogue of thank you letters received from soldiers, which is growing all the time. "The letters we receive are humbling: one even apologised for his bad writing due to having almost lost his eyesight. Of course, these young men are the ones to be thanked."

In December 2013, MR PORTER and Ms Emma Willis co-hosted the Style For Soldiers Christmas party in London. In the run-up to this annual event, we spoke to six ex-servicemen who have benefited from the charitable incentive's work.

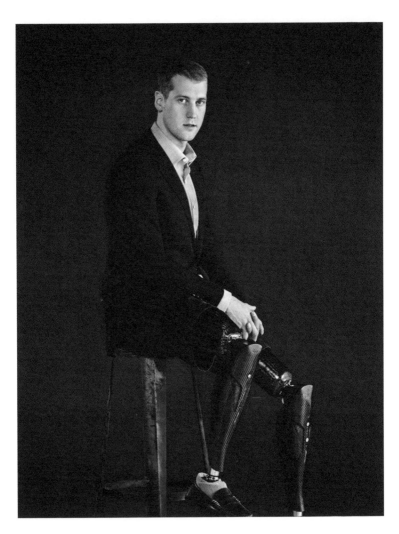

CAPT. GARTH BANKS, 31
1st Battalion Grenadier Guards

Captain Garth Banks was a Platoon Commander in the
1st Battalion Grenadier Guards. In January 2010, while on patrol
in Afghanistan, he stepped on an IED (improvised explosive
device). He lost both of his legs above the knee.

"I don't come from a military background. I wanted to challenge myself and thought that this was the way to do it. I joined up in September 2007 and spent a year at Sandhurst Royal Military Academy, followed by training for Afghanistan and eventual deployment in September 2009.

"I was put into an induced coma after the blast. During those six days my mind must have subconsciously come to terms with what had happened, because by the time I woke up in hospital in Birmingham I'd already accepted the fact that I'd lost my legs and felt quite aware of the consequences for my future. I'm stoical about it, I suppose, but I think that's a natural human reaction. When something like this happens, you just have to get on with it.

"I've been in and out of Headley Court ever since my injury. During one stay, someone mentioned that a nice woman and her attractive assistant were coming to visit and that if anyone wanted a bespoke shirt she'd measure you up. I thought, you can't say no, can you? Emma's a firecracker, she's got so much energy. She just makes things happen. Style For Soldiers makes a real difference. These kind of injuries can affect the way you perceive yourself. You're not the same and you'll never be the same, but certain things haven't changed. You still want to look smart. It's still important – maybe even more so, and Emma has realised that.

"I leave the army in January [2014], so that'll be the end of that period of my life, and I'm looking at what to do next. I like the idea of doing something in the Paralympics. There's a possibility that I might be able to play tennis, as I played a lot before, and I'm hoping to see a development coach in the next couple of weeks to see how viable this is."

CAPT. STUART CROXFORD, 29
1st Battalion The Duke of Lancaster's Regiment

Captain Stuart Croxford served in The Duke of Lancaster's Regiment as the Reconnaissance Platoon Commander. During his second tour of Afghanistan, his vehicle drove over an IED while serving with the Brigade Reconnaissance Force in Helmand Province. The blast caused severe damage to both feet.

"I went to Manchester University to train as an architect. At the time, I didn't want to be in the army. My father was – still is, in fact. I wasn't railing against it as such, I just wanted to do something else. It was only later, during my part two work placement, that I changed my mind and decided to give the whole thing a go while I was still young, before it was too late. I ended up stationed in Catterick Garrison in the northeast, 20 minutes from my parents' place. Typical – you join up to travel the world, and you get sent back to where you grew up.

"Getting injured was an eye-opener. Sat there in a hospital bed and going from being a Reconnaissance Platoon Commander in Afghanistan to being unable to manage anything for myself was a big shock. I'm a very independent person, and having that snatched away so quickly was hard to take.

"I met Emma at Headley Court quite early on, while I was still in a wheelchair. In a room full of people, all her focus would be on you. We spoke about a few things while I was being measured up, and she emailed me back the next day mentioning specific details of our conversation, recommending people that I could talk to for work experience and mentoring. Multiply this by the 30, 40 guys that she must have measured that day alone, and the level of attention and care is incredible. It brings out the best in the guys who are lacking in confidence.

"I've got a medical discharge out of the army in January 2015, and I'm waiting on further operations. The aim is to get me walking pain free, and I'd be happy with that. I was always a keen sportsman. I loved rugby and I used to do triathlons, and that's probably out of the question now, but getting back into skiing is a massive goal for me – there's an MOD initiative called Battle Back that focuses on adaptive sport, it's a great opportunity to refocus your aspirations and try new sports."

CAPT. ALEX HORSFALL, 31
2nd Battalion The Rifles

Captain Alex Horsfall was a Platoon Commander in the 2nd
Battalion The Rifles. He lost his left leg and half of his left hand in
a bomb blast in Sangin, Helmand in June 2010 on what was
the bloodiest day of the Afghan conflict for British troops.

"I grew up on Salisbury Plain. Stonehenge area. I suppose that's where I first developed an intrigue into the army, living next to this enormous military training estate. Planes flying overhead, artillery going off: we had a dog who'd spend most of its life under a table. Sometimes we'd go up onto the plain on a quad bike and pick up the old bits of debris that the army had left behind.

"I spent four months in Sangin, Helmand province. It's a very claustrophobic town, full of narrow alleyways and big, high walls. IED heaven. Everything was going rather well, but all you really need is five minutes when things aren't going to plan. We ended up in a blast that killed five of the soldiers in my platoon and injured six or seven others.

"I woke up six days later in a hospital bed in Birmingham a little bit baffled, but then I was high on ketamine, and God knows what else. I'd lost my leg there and then, but because of phantom feelings, I'd wake up and still be able to feel it. I can still feel it now. So when they told me that I'd lost it, I just assumed it was some sort of administrative error. As far as I was aware, I just had a hole in my mattress and the leg was dangling through. It took a while for it all to sink in. Even two weeks later, I still hadn't realised that I was no longer in command. In the hospital in the middle of the night I'd dream that I was still in Afghanistan and nobody could hear me barking orders.

"Pride is hardly something that the military lack, but it can take a dent in these circumstances. What really helps you to get it back is when you return to civilian life and encounter support and compassion from the general public. This is something that has quite drastically improved in the past 10 years, and what Emma does with Style For Soldiers is a great example. There is a definite correlation between how smartly you're dressed and the pride with which you carry yourself."

RESERVE TROOPER ADAM COCKS, 31
Honourable Artillery Company
(attached to 4/73 Special of Battery)

Reserve Trooper Adam Cocks was an investment consultant in the City of London when he joined the Territorial Army as part of the Honourable Artillery Company. He received serious leg injuries in a double IED blast in Afghanistan in January 2008.

"My first day in the City was 11 September 2001. I was doing work experience, and I still remember the chaos. A few years later in 2005, on the day that London was attacked, I was in a hotel right next to Aldgate East, near one of the tube stops that was hit. When you see these things they do have an impact, and I guess I felt compelled to do something. Queen and country all the way, I'm afraid. It might be a bit old-fashioned, but that's the way it affects me.

"It was 20 January 2008 – we were blown up twice within 20 minutes. We'd driven our vehicles into cover during the night in advance of a foot patrol. It was cold overnight and the ground was frozen. What we didn't realise was that we'd driven into a minefield. Come morning, the ground had thawed and the vehicles' wheels had sunk lower. I was driving when the first blast went off. I took some shrapnel to the nose, and I remember being covered in curry. We had our rations on the bonnet and they went everywhere. The second blast blew me out of the vehicle.

"I'd fractured my knee in various places as well as other multiple injuries. To make things worse, in July 2008 I was travelling from my medals parade in North Yorkshire to a hospital in Frimley, Surrey when I was involved in a road traffic accident that caused further damage to the injured leg. I've now got a metal hip, thigh and knee. They say things come in threes – well, that's mine.

"It's taken nearly three and a half years of rehabilitation, but from where I stand now, after being told in 2008 that I'd never bend my leg, I feel like I've come a long way. I can walk, and don't always use a stick – even though, thanks to Emma, I have a very nice one now. I can't run, but I can swim. I'm very fortunate. After being medically discharged and briefly returning to my job in the City, I was recently able to take on a new opportunity outside of the finance world. It's goodbye to the 12-hour days chained to a chair. I can appreciate life, take Dougal [his dog] for walks. Things are good."

CAPT. EDMUND ADDINGTON, 30
2nd Battalion The Rifles

Captain Edmund Addington, a farmer's son from Wiltshire, served in Iraq, Northern Ireland and Kosovo before being severely injured in a blast in Afghanistan in 2009.

"On 27 September 2009 on Route 611 in Sangin I should have been killed. I was in an open-top vehicle in the commander's seat, the passenger side. The explosion went off right underneath me and threw me from the vehicle. It was a 19-year-old female medic who left the scene and went out beyond our position – a very risky thing to do – and found me.

"I was slumped against a wall with a head injury, an eye injury, a shattered left arm, a collapsed left lung, a broken back L1 to 4, my right ankle was exposed, my left foot had been what they call 'degloved', and I had severe frag to my hip… suffice to say, that initial treatment didn't give the best of prognoses. Medical experience gained in the past six months in Afghanistan certainly saved my life; I have no doubt that it saved my limbs. I look at my injuries and I think how very lucky I've been. So many colleagues have not come back, so who am I to worry for one second?

"I spent three months in hospital followed by three years of intensive rehab at Headley Court. To date, I've had 20 operations. From tour to treatment to rehab, it has occasionally been hard to escape the bubble of being an injured soldier. You don't know what's going on outside, and I wasn't sure if the rest of the world understood or even knew what was happening in Afghanistan. When Emma arrived, it sent a message that there are people outside of your immediate environment who care about the sacrifices that you've made. That is hugely valuable when you're fighting a tough mental and physical battle.

"Physically, my goals were to be able to use public transport and go up steps. If you can do that, you have a lot of options open to you. I've been very fortunate to recover enough to be able to do that. Professionally, I work in consulting now and I want to take my military experience and military values and put them to good use in the commercial world."

CAPT. JAMES MURLY-GOTTO, 30
Scots Guards

Captain James Murly-Gotto studied at Eton and Oxford before joining the Scots Guards. In 2010, while taking part in Operation Moshtarak in Afghanistan, he was hit in both legs in a friendly fire incident. He nearly lost his right leg as a result of his injuries.

"Like a lot of people from army families, I suppose I was brought up on tales of my father's adventures – or misadventures, should I say. I joined the army because I thought it seemed like a good idea to go and have a few of my own.

"We'd been in Afghanistan for just under a month when I was hit. We'd managed to weather 10 days of ferocious fighting and had called the heli to take us back to base. It was dark, and we were marking the landing site. I remember realising that it was friendly fire when I saw the red laser range finder. 'The Taliban don't use one of those,' I thought. A round hit me in my right shinbone and tracked upwards, popping out of the knee – it cleaved off about a quarter of the leg.

"I'm obviously very lucky to still have the thing, but I'd be lying if I said that I wasn't without inhibition. I am conscious of my injury. I have quite a large scar which is susceptible to sunlight and burns easily, so I suppose I'm lucky to live here in London where we're not blessed with too much sunshine and I can get away with wearing trousers most of the year.

"Back in WWII, there was a hospital in Sussex set up to deal with downed RAF pilots who'd suffered horrendous facial burns. They called the guys The Guinea Pig Club, on account of the rather experimental plastic surgery they underwent. Some of the results weren't pretty, but they were encouraged to go out into society anyway. At the pub, the hospital staff would prep the locals to treat them like anyone else, and it helped to condition them back into the normal world.

"What Style For Soldiers does is similar, in a way. When Emma comes into Headley Court and measures you up, she doesn't judge because someone's missing an arm. She'll measure them up just the same as she would any of her customers on Jermyn Street. What she does is to help injured soldiers feel like normal people. And when ex-soldiers arc entering back into civilian life, a good shirt that fits you perfectly can be just the suit of armour that you need."

TEN GREAT ADVENTURE READS

*One spirited traveller shares the tomes that inspired
him to cycle 46,000 miles across the globe*

Words by Mr Alastair Humphreys

I READ MY FIRST Ranulph Fiennes book when I should have been revising for my A levels. By the time I sat university final exams I was a lost case, buried deep in Ernest Shackleton, Eric Newby and Bill Tilman. I was hooked on adventure books, great stories of endeavour and hardship played out against a backdrop of the wildest landscapes on earth. I needed more of this. I needed some of it for myself. So I climbed onto my bike and set off to test myself out there in the world's wild places. I spent four years cycling 46,000 miles around the world, but this didn't slake my thirst. I've written books of my own now and chased adventure to the ends of the earth. But adventure, and adventure's great canon of literature, is like Pandora's box. Open the box and you're cursed forever. There are more landscapes and adventures than you can fit into one lifetime, and more great tales of adventure too. I hope that these 10 favourites of mine, picked to encompass a variety of styles of adventure, will get you itching for new horizons and the spell of the open road.

I
THE WORST JOURNEY IN THE WORLD
Apsley Cherry-Garrard

An unoriginal entrant in a list of great adventure books, but with good reason. This is the official account of Captain Robert Falcon Scott's fateful final expedition to the South Pole (and a smaller, offshoot trip to collect some penguin eggs, which is unimaginably hardcore and grim). The prose is poetic, the characters are heroic, stoic and dignified. Humanity and humour shine through, and few can read the final page without a tear. Extraordinary adventures at the end of the world, acted out by phenomenal men, and written phenomenally well: this is why it's on everyone's list.

2
ARABIAN SANDS
Wilfred Thesiger

Arabian Sands is another acknowledged "great" adventure book. Wilfred Thesiger's brave, ascetic journeys in the vast, intimidating, silent Empty Quarter desert are recounted in sparse prose. Thesiger admires the tough, nomadic Bedouin people he travelled alongside and mourns the encroachment of modernity into their lives and his own. For a more general overview of his great life, consider *The Life of My Choice* instead.

3
WIND, SAND AND STARS
Antoine de Saint-Exupéry

This is a beautiful, engrossing story filled with gems of wisdom about life and the human experience. It's also a hell of an adventure. The author was a pilot, flying mail routes from France, across the Pyrenees and the Sahara desert, back in the days when this was phenomenally difficult and dangerous to do. At one point, he crashes and almost dies before being rescued in the desert. Beautiful and dramatic in equal measure.

4
NO PICNIC ON MOUNT KENYA
Felice Benuzzi

A more light-hearted mountaineering book, but no less inspiring. *No Picnic on Mount Kenya* tells the tale of three Italian prisoners of war whose camp is in Kenya. Gazing up at the mountain reminds them of all the adventure and freedom they've lost. So they decide to escape, solely in order to try to climb Mount Kenya. They must make their own climbing equipment, escape from prison and then attempt the first ever ascent of the mountain. If you mixed *The Great Escape* with a beautifully narrated mountaineering book and ode to freedom, then this is the tale you'd get.

5
THE KON-TIKI EXPEDITION
Thor Heyerdahl

Continuing with wild and wonderfully eccentric adventure books, *The Kon-Tiki Expedition* is an absolute classic. Thor Heyerdahl believed that Polynesia could have been settled by people from

South America crossing the Pacific Ocean on balsawood rafts. Tired of being told it was impossible, he set out to prove that it could be done. In an age before satellite phones and GPS-tracked emergency lifeboats, this was an adventure that was truly reckless, remote and dangerous. But Heyerdahl and his mates were so tough that they even resorted to catching sharks by hand for a little light entertainment mid-voyage.

6

SAILING ALONE AROUND THE WORLD
Joshua Slocum

This account of the first man to sail solo around the world is still popular and relevant for adventurous souls today. Written more than 100 years ago at the end of the great age of sail, Joshua Slocum's story feels like an end-of-era adventure. In those pre-Facebook days, being away from home for three years was like disappearing to another world. Arthur Ransome, the author of *Swallows and Amazons*, loved the book, declaring boldly that "boys who do not like this book ought to be drowned at once".

7

MOONDUST
Andrew Smith

More remote even than sailing solo around the world a century ago is the idea of standing on the moon. Surely mankind's greatest ever adventure, the sheer concept of blasting almost a quarter of a million miles away into space is both preposterous and fabulous. Only 12 people have ever stood on the moon and *Moondust* is the author's attempt to interview these now old men before it's too late. An extraordinary tale of hubris, ingenuity and good old-fashioned adventure.

TRAVELS WITH CHARLEY
John Steinbeck

At around the same time as America was trying to blast a man off to the moon, an almost 60-year-old John Steinbeck set off with his dog Charley to drive round his country and try to take stock of his own life and his fast-changing surroundings. This is a sedate adventure (there's lots of pottering around, eating baked beans and drinking whisky) but it's humorous, sad and filled with curiosity and all the fine writing you'd expect from Steinbeck.

9
ANNAPURNA
Maurice Herzog

Mountaineering exerts a heavy toll on its disciples. Perhaps that's why climbing so often makes for great adventure books. *Annapurna* is no different. It has everything you'd expect in a good climbing book: derring-do, misery, frostbite. A beautifully written and honest book, *Annapurna* tells the tale of the first-ever ascent of an 8,000m mountain. What a story! But what a cost!

10
AS I WALKED OUT ONE MIDSUMMER MORNING
Laurie Lee

Laurie Lee inspired generations of vagabonds with this beautiful little book. He leaves his village home and walks to London to earn enough cash for a one-way ferry ticket to Spain. Disembarking with only enough Spanish to "ask for a glass of water", he sets out to walk the length of Spain, earning money en route by busking with his violin. This is a spontaneous, lyrical coming-of-age adventure.

GEORGE CLEVERLEY

We meet the men at Britain's finest bespoke shoemaker

Words by Mr Mansel Fletcher

WHILE TAILORING AFICIONADOS are often to be found vigorously debating the relative merits of Savile Row suits vis-à-vis Neapolitan suits, it's uncontroversial to say that the best men's shoes are made in England. Among the British brands there are a handful of bespoke shoemakers still producing traditional handmade shoes, of which George Cleverley stands pre-eminent.

More than 90 years ago, the late Mr George Cleverley dedicated himself to the creation of the finest shoes in the world, and he worked until his death at the age of 92. As a child he sold bootlaces and shoe polish and later worked in a British Army boot factory during WWI. In 1920 he joined Tuczek, a famous Mayfair shoemaker, before setting up on his own as a bespoke maker in 1958. In the same year Mr Cleverley's nephew Mr Anthony Cleverley also left Tuczek and set up on his own as a bespoke shoemaker.

After the death of Mr George Cleverley in 1991, Mr George Glasgow and last-maker Mr John Carnera, who had worked alongside Mr Cleverley since 1978, were asked to carry on the business. Mr Glasgow has been the managing director ever since, and he opened the current shop in London's Royal Arcade on Old Bond Street. When Mr Anthony Cleverley died, his niece asked Mr Glasgow and Mr Carnera to take on his mantle and combine the designs and history of these two great shoemakers.

"George [Cleverley] told me that his nephew was a wonderful shoemaker, but that he couldn't get on with him at all, so they never spoke," explains Mr Glasgow. As a result, the two Mr Cleverleys worked in parallel, but separately; Mr George Cleverley was a society shoemaker with a shop in Mayfair while his nephew worked from home in north London for a small, but exclusive, group of clients.

According to Mr Glasgow, Mr Anthony Cleverley only accepted new customers if they were introduced by an existing client, a policy that created a list of names including Baron Alexis de Redé, Mr Mark Birley, a few Rothschilds and a Forte or two. To that group, Mr George Cleverley added Messrs Rudolph Valentino, Gary Cooper and Clark Gable, a couple of English dukes and a member of the British royal family. Today the author Mr Tom Wolfe and Rolling Stone Mr Charlie Watts are devoted customers.

Messrs George Glasgow Sr (co-owner and chairman) and George Glasgow Jr (co-owner and CEO) in their London workshop

EIGHT WAYS TO LOOK FRESH
FOR THE OFFICE

*Only a few small changes and you'll look
twice as nice and half as old*

Words by Ms Jodie Harrison

WHILE WE WOULD NEVER WANT you to become an anti-ageing obsessive, there is something to be said for a bit of undercover preservation. After all, if you are going to spend a sizeable chunk of your time and income on dressing well, you might as well keep everything else looking good too. Not only that, looking your best has become an integral part of keeping a firm grip on the career ladder. The good news is that no matter how fortunately or unfortunately you may think you are ageing, there's always something that can be done to make the most of what's left. With this in mind, we highlight a few steps to help any man give Old Mother Time a run for her money.

1

IF IT'S GOING, SHAVE IT

There's no point getting sentimental about receding hair. If it's on its way out, cut loose and start over. If it's your first stab at shaving your head, it's best to see a professional. The time of year to carry out the act can also be key – we'd suggest shaving it during a two-week holiday in the sun. That way it won't look as if you are wearing a fleshy water polo cap on your head.

2

WEAR THE CORRECT UNDERWEAR

On a recent (and let's say accidental) visit to a famous nudist beach on the island of Formentera last summer, I became unwillingly introduced to a physical phenomenon that an American writer of ours, Mr Jordan Kaye, had described to me casually over breakfast several months back: middle-aged ball droop. "It's something that will affect all of us at a certain age," explained Mr Kaye mid-mouthful of eggs Benedict, "but wearing the right underwear apparently helps." Supportive underwear (ie, snug-fitting knitted types rather than billowing cotton jobs) has never seemed so appealing...

3
MICRO-MANAGE THE SIGNS

"Age? It's the one mountain you can't overcome," said 81-year-old comedian and plastic surgery mascot Ms Joan Rivers. She's right of course (not that it stopped an impressive attempt at the summit), but there are small things that can be done every year that won't hurt your self-esteem. "Skin tone is really the hallmark of good, young skin," explains Dr Tapan Patel, a London-based aesthetician known for his laser work in the field of non-surgical anti-ageing procedures. "Very early signs of ageing, although seemingly unnoticeable, can be dealt with quickly to prevent longer-term ageing issues such as severe thread veins and a sagging jaw line." Thanks to new laser breeds, thread veins (the tiny red veins that usually congregate on your nose and cheeks somewhere during your mid- to late thirties) can now be removed quickly and relatively pain-free with very little, and often zero, recovery time using a V-beam laser. Treat them in small doses now and there will be a lot less work to do later, he advises.

4
TAKE A SIZE DOWN

You look older in clothes that don't fit properly. It really is as simple as that. Loose fits may have suited you in your youth, where ripe young flesh is able to ripple through sack-like fits, but in later life, excess fabric just adds pounds on a generally pound-sufficient age group. "Fit is something we get the most queries about," says Mr John Buckley, Sales and Customer Care Assistant Manager for MR PORTER. "A lot of men wear pieces that are too big for them and it's always such a pleasure to hear how dropping down a size makes them feel so much younger and smarter."

5
WHITEN-UP, STRAIGHTEN-UP

You like a cup of coffee, as well as a glass of red wine – and we at MR PORTER appreciate that – but such small vices can really smear your deal-sealing, smile campaign in the long run. Rather than get into the habit of staining then whitening, wouldn't it be better to continually address the issue via your daily brushing regime? Enter the Philips Sonicare DiamondClean, which was shown in clinical trials to not only polish, remove stains and plaque within two weeks, but also whiten teeth in one week. It even comes with its own charging glass – a natty little gadget that uses hi-tech conduction technology to charge the brush while it rests in a glass by your sink. This thing is the Bugatti of toothbrushes.

6
LOSE WEIGHT, LOSE YEARS

Carrying weight around your middle is a serious sign not only of your age but of your declining health. Stress causes the body to store fat in this area, so it's a common sight among over-worked City-types. Introducing a cleaner diet (lots of protein, nuts, berries and healthy fats) is one of the best anti-ageing solutions out there, and one that Bodyism founder Mr James Duigan (one of London's top trainers) has based his whole life around. Combined with training, his range of daily supplements and shakes will potentially help you carve out a whole new, younger-looking version of yourself.

7
CHANGE YOUR SHOE SHAPE

No matter how well you hide your age, your shoe choice can be a giveaway to any discerning onlooker (read: female). Choosing to wear the same shoe shape you wore in your youth isn't always the answer to looking younger. Your shoes won't lie. As your looks change, so should your shoe shape.

THE GOLDILOCKS SCALE
OF SHOE CHOICES

POINTY: too young. No one wants to see a grown man in cheap shoes, worn till the toe point buckles and creases northwards while paired with a suit.

ROUND: often very ageing unless you are in your twenties, particularly with a suit. Bulbous brogues can make feet look stumpy and clumsy, so choose wisely. The trick in your older years is to dress your feet up to look more elegant in shape, rather than to accentuate any stubbiness.

LONG, LEAN: ah, just right. Helps continue the clean and elegant lines of your perfectly tailored jacket.

MAINTAIN YOUR EYEBROWS

Like the skin on your hands, your eyebrows can be a sure-fire signal of advancing age. As you get older, they get bigger, bushier and harder to maintain. Leave them to their own devices and you risk looking on the wrong side of eccentric. "Men generally develop more hair as they become older, and eyebrows are no exception. Grey hair is also coarser, which adds to the problem," says Ms Priya Kerai, senior brow architect (yes, really) at international eyebrow emporium Browhaus. "The trick is to keep them neat without appearing overly groomed." The solutions available are as wide as you are willing. Ms Kerai suggests letting a professional like herself take control by booking in for one of her "thread and tweeze" signature treatments every four to six weeks. If you'd prefer to keep this between you and your brows, we'd suggest buying a good pair of tweezers and using a comb to brush the hairs backwards, trimming any strays at a slight angle (try Tweezerman's mini slant tweezers and keep a spare pair in your top drawer at work). Finish with an eyebrow fixing gel or wax, such as Givenchy's Mister Eyebrow (designed specifically for men), to keep them all in place.

ACKNOWLEDGMENTS

Editor-in-Chief – Mr John Brodie
Creative Director – Mr Leon St-Amour
Editor – Ms Jodie Harrison
Production Director – Ms Xanthe Greenhill
Style Director – Mr Dan May
Designer – Mr Eric Åhnebrink
Chief Sub-Editor – Ms Siân Morgan
Deputy Sub-Editor – Mr James Coulson
Picture Editor – Ms Katie Morgan
Editorial Assistant – Ms Caroline Hogan

CONTRIBUTORS

Ms Marie Belmoh, Mr Rik Burgess, Mr Jacopo Maria Cinti,
Mr Tony Cook, Ms Laura Cumming, Mr Chris Elvidge,
Mr Tom M Ford, Mr Patrick Guilfoyle,
Ms Sophie Hardcastle, Mr Tom Harris, Mr Daniel Koch,
Mr Lewis Malpas, Mr David Pearson, Ms Jessica Ruiz,
Ms Rachael Smart, Mr Scott Stephenson, Mr Ian Tansley,
Mr Angelo Trofa

With thanks to
Ms Natalie Massenet

CREDITS

1-2 Vincent Mahe; 6 Blair Getz Mezibov; 13-14 Courtesy Porsche; 16-25 John Balsom; 28-32 Peden + Munk; 35 Hulton Archive/ Getty Images; 36 Matt Irwin; 39 Paul Schutzer/ The LIFE Picture Collection/ Getty Images; 40 © 1978 David Sutton/ mptvimages.com; 41 Hulton Archive/ Getty Images; 42t © Raymond Depardon/ Magnum Photos; 42b NBC/ NBCU Photo Bank via Getty Images; 43 John Dominis/ Time & Life Pictures/ Getty Images; 44 François Pages/ Paris Match via Getty Images; 45 Antony Hare; 48-50 Benjamin McMahon; 52 Tony Roberts/ Corbis; 53 Courtesy The Royal County Down Golf Club; 54 Courtesy Bandon Dunes Golf Resort; 55 David Cannon/ Getty Images; 56 Courtesy Club de Golf Valderrama; 59 David Lees/ The LIFE Picture Collection/ Getty Images; 60 John Dominis/ Time & Life Pictures/ Getty Images; 61 Tim Graham/ Getty Images; 62 Jean-Pierre BONNOTTE/ Gamma-Rapho via Getty Images; 63 Imagno/ Getty Images; 64-68 Linda Brownlee c/o East Photographic; 71 Robert Anzell/ Rex Features; 72 George Strock/ Time & Life Pictures/ Getty Images; 73 Giorgio Lotti/ Mondadori Portfolio by Getty Images; 74 Silver Screen Collection/ Getty Images; 75 mptvimages.com; 76 © Philippe Halsman/ Magnum Photos; 77 Douglas Jones, LOOK Magazine/ John F Kennedy Presidential Library and Museum, Boston; 78 Archivio Cameraphoto Epoche/ Getty Images; 79 Sipa Press/ Rex Features; 80 Slim Aarons/ Getty Images; 81 © Henri Cartier-Bresson/ Magnum Photos; 82 Bob Willoughby/ Getty Images; 83 © Martine

MR PORTER is the global online retail
destination for men's style,
offering more than 200 of the world's
leading menswear brands.

Visit MRPORTER.COM